THE HEART
is the
STRONGEST
MUSCLE

KNOW YOUR WHY AND TAKE YOUR MINDSET FROM GREAT TO UNSTOPPABLE

RODALE

NEW YORK

THE HEART

is the

STRONGEST MUSCLE

TIA-CLAIR TOOMEY-ORR

Library of Congress Cataloging-in-Publication Data
is on file with the publisher.

ISBN 978-0-593-57961-9
Ebook ISBN 978-0-593-57962-6

Printed in the United States of America

Book design by Andrea Lau
Jacket design: Caroline Johnson
Jacket photograph: Courtesy of CrossFit, LLC
Author photograph: Courtesy of Nobull

10 9 8 7 6 5 4 3 2 1

First Edition

To Shane, Willow, and the rest of my family

CONTENTS

A Note from the Author

This book is for anyone who really wants to change their life. It is not for someone who is looking for excuses or unwilling to go full tilt in unleashing their potential. I am going to be straight with you throughout these pages, because the advice is that simple and that black and white. There is no gray area when it comes to winning.

INTRODUCTION

I never started CrossFit to become one of the most dominant athletes of all time. The goal at first was likely similar to yours—to simply help me get fitter—but it has done way more than that. My path over the years has allowed me to evolve as a person, as everything I have learned in the gym has applied in my daily life. And the biggest lesson in being a champion isn't just about gold medals. It's really about the journey—and all the blood, sweat, and tears that go into it.

This became very apparent after I came in second for the second time at the CrossFit Games in 2016. After that disappointing experience, I realized that I needed to understand what I was missing; it wasn't the *physical* aspect I brought to the floor. I was good there. But I realized that I had not yet fully engaged the right mindset I needed to commit 100 percent to becoming unstoppable. That was the moment when I needed to choose my path: Was CrossFit going to be my future or just a stepping stone?

I found myself thinking about something my dad had said to me when I was a little girl growing up on the Sunshine Coast of Australia: "You always need to feed your mind." When he said that, I was so young I thought he meant literally feeding the brain with real food. I now know better, of course, and I know that he meant my body can physically keep going all day, every day, but I also have to train my mind. If I neglected that, I would hold myself back. The body is built to do incredible things, but the mind and the heart determine how far you will go.

I had always brought the hard work and given my absolute best, but I had to figure out how to better apply my mental fortitude to my advantage. So, I did what anyone would do—I began to read books and listen to podcasts about mental performance. There is a saying that we have two ears and one mouth so that we can listen twice as much as we speak (even though I could talk all day long). I read everything I could get my hands on and listened to all the experts, and while this did provide some great inspiration, nothing taught me the secret of getting on top of the podium. However, it did help provide reassurance that I was on the right track. It also helped me understand why I felt the way I did, as I began to better understand the processes that were already happening to me when I was training and competing.

Shane—my husband and coach—and I didn't know it at the time, but we were on a path to making me unstoppable. Looking back now, while being physically dominant is certainly part of it, moving from being great at CrossFit to unstoppable required a relentless commitment from the body, mind, and heart. Anyone from the amateur athlete to the elite professional knows what I am talking about—that indescribable fire in the belly that gets you out of bed at 5 a.m. every day to work out for years (and years upon years). People can argue over whether or not someone is talented or focused enough, but if they don't have that workhorse mentality to keep the grind going, everything else falls apart. Throughout my time competing in the CrossFit Games, the 2016 Rio Olympics, the 2018 Commonwealth Games, as well as qualifying for a spot in the 2022 Olympics two-woman bobsled team, my road to success has not been easy. I have hit lots of walls, roadblocks, hurdles—whatever metaphor you choose—but what has gotten me through it all is my recalibrated focus and never losing my heart in the game. You can train your mind and body to be a machine, but if your heart isn't in it, you might as well pack it in and call it a day.

Anyone can give you a workout schedule and say, "Hey, do this and you'll be competing with the rest of us," but that isn't how the game is won. True success comes from your heart and your head, not just your physical performance. Obviously, you need to physically be able to do a lot of things, but if you aren't committed and you don't mentally prepare, then your physical ability is only going to get you so far. What you are holding in your hands is the blueprint to how I became unstoppable—and how you can, too.

THE HEART
is the
STRONGEST
MUSCLE

CHAPTER 1

Keep the Heart Beating

Finding Your Why and Keeping the Momentum

I grew up on a sugarcane farm near Dunethin Rock, which sits along the Maroochy River on the Sunshine Coast about 60 miles north of Brisbane, Australia. While my home was just a few miles outside of town, it might as well have been a thousand miles away. To get to school, I'd often canoe or boat off the beautiful lush riverbank in front of our property to a neighboring farm, where I could then catch the school bus. After school, the undeveloped bush that was my backyard would be my playground, where I'd ride my motorbike, play ball with my dogs, and swim in the rolling, saltwater river. From a young age, my parents encouraged me to expend that energy in many different avenues, from taking up music—I went from playing piano to the guitar to the drums—to all kinds of sports. At one point,

I played a different sport every afternoon after school, but I took to running the most. It was the training runs that made me understand how important it was to have a strong foundation and work hard for something. I loved the simplicity of being so incredibly physical without any prop or equipment. It felt so freeing to just take off on my own. I also liked the individualism of it: that you are responsible for your success alone (even though it was as much a team effort with my mum and dad helping me along the way).

"I really want to see how far I can go with my running," I blurted out to my parents one night at the dinner table. I was about 11 at the time. "I want to represent Queensland (our state) at Nationals."

"Okay, Tia, we're going to have to work hard and you're the one who's going to have to get up early in the morning, and you're going to have to do training sessions in the afternoon . . ." my dad said. My mum added, "And when your friends ask you to go over for sleepovers, you're going to have to say no, because you're going to have to train on the weekends . . ."

"Yup, got it!" I answered enthusiastically and looked back at them with steel-eyed determination. From that day on, I had support from my parents—never too much, never too little—which gave me an amazing space in which to develop and grow. I woke up at 5 a.m. to hit the pool every single morning (my dad was big on cross-training) and trained when I got home from school. Every. Single. Day. I am sure a lot of people thought, *Whoa, why are her parents grinding her when she's so young*? But it was all me. I was the one getting my dad up and bugging him that we had to go. Don't get me wrong, there were definitely mornings where I would whine groggily at my dad, "Just a few more minutes of sleep . . ."

"Well, if you want to make it to Nationals, this is what it takes, Tia."

I knew he was right.

I had my first major cross-country competition at age 11, and I was so incredibly nervous. At that age, it seemed that the other runners had so much more experience than me and here I was just making my debut. But I placed third on that first meet, and I told my dad incredulously, "Dad, I think I could actually *win* at this stuff!"

My motivation went into overdrive after placing third, as I continued competing. My dad was my first coach. He had been an athlete himself—he had competed regionally in swimming and football (*soccer* to you Americans)—so he knew how to pump me up before a meet. He would shout encouragement from the sidelines, such as, "Come on, Tia. Show me how big your heart is!" My mum was always there, too, standing next to him, cheering me on. This helped me get to the finish line, proud and clean, knowing that I had given it my absolute all. From an early age, I knew my heart was the strongest muscle; I knew that my success relied not just on physical ability and grit, but passion. Passion is what keeps me going—I didn't need any fancy facility or the best running shoes to give me power. That was already deep down inside me.

And, back then, as today, I wear my heart on my sleeve. When I cross the finish line, I instinctively let out an emotional roar and raise my fists in the air, letting it all out. All this passion and drive always, always, always goes back to the "why."

Know Your Why

Everyone needs a why in his or her life—a mission statement, a purpose, a deep motivation that fuels you. The why feeds into everything you do. Ask yourself: Why do you want to run a marathon, play soccer, or, like me, win CrossFit Games over and over again? Is it to be at the top of your game in your profession? Is it to be the best person you can be? Is it to leave a legacy for your kids? Or is it to achieve financial security? Once you understand what your why is, then everything falls into place. In fact, absolutely every other key concept in this book is secondary and won't work unless you understand this. Shane—as he's my husband and coach, you'll be reading a lot about him in these pages!—likes to visualize two concentric circles: The inner circle is your why and everything that is outside the circle represents all decisions based on that why. For instance, will going out for drinks on the weekend get me closer to my goal of making the CrossFit Games? Probably not. Or if I go for a swim with my friends on the weekend, will that get me in fighting form? Well, it is better than going out drinking, but it's still probably not the best use of my time. I am sure there are a lot of places in your life where you could cut out the fat once you pose the why question. When it comes to those hard obstacles and facing adversity on a daily basis, your commitment to your why will always determine your actions; it will determine whether or not you're going to take the easy or the hard option.

When I first started in earnest with CrossFit, Shane and I had been together for a number of years and had been having conversations about when we were going to start our family. We both felt very strongly about wanting kids one day. So my why was this: I want to be a parent who has stories to tell her kids, stories that show if they want to go out and achieve something, they can do anything they put their mind to. I wanted to create my own story first, one that could, in turn, provide hope and inspiration for my future family, so that they could grow up and absolutely crush whatever it is that they wanted to accomplish, whether it was in sports, arts, business, or marine biology.

Why am I telling you all this? To show that while everyone can have motivation, finding your why is much more important for long-lasting results. Everyone can have motivation for five minutes, but that can run low pretty quickly. Motivation is temporary. But knowing your why will give you momentum, which is much more long-lasting. Shane defines *momentum* as a series of habits that help you build consistency in your training. I think that people are always just looking for the quick gratification and hoping motivation gets them across that line. It may give you enough zing to make a 30-second workout reel on Instagram, but it's not going to get you up at 5 a.m. to run in the rain for hours.

And this is where it's important to understand the difference between motivation and momentum. Motivation is the desire to achieve a goal or a result; you need momentum to keep motivation up. Think of motivation as that boost to get you on the bike and start peddling, but it is your momentum that keeps you peddling. Motivation *gets* you going, but momentum is what you *keeps* you going.

Motivation Can Ebb and Flow Like the Tide—and That Is Good

We moved to Weipa, a small town about 1,500 miles north of Brisbane, when I was 14, but I continued training. I kept getting better, faster, and stronger, accumulating awards every year, from 2004 to 2010. Shane came into my life when I was about 15—we met at a triathlon. We began our friendship through our love of sports. He started helping out with my training before and after school, taking over stopwatch duty when my dad was working. So that's where it all started. (It's funny to reflect now how Shane embraced the role of being my coach even back then!)

In 2009, my parents made the decision to enroll me in boarding school for my last two years of high school. It was located in Townsville, a 16-hour drive south of Weipa, on the coast of Queensland. The first 12 weeks away from home were the hardest. I was incredibly homesick and cried myself to sleep nearly every night, but I used that loneliness to keep me going.

Compared to Weipa, I had so many more opportunities at my fingertips, from training partners to more modern facilities to working out in the morning and swimming in the Olympic-sized pool, and running after my classes in the afternoon (on an actual athletic track, not the makeshift grass track at my old school).

Even though my parents were hundreds of miles away, my dad would be in my head, always encouraging me. His pep talks—what I imagined them to be—helped me keep going. The time on my own reinforced the fact that I wanted this for myself, especially since I didn't have the crutch of my dad getting me up at 5 a.m. or timing me on my run. This time taught me that I had the will and the desire and the determination needed to do this—I had to rely on myself. I also knew how much they were investing in me and I didn't want to let them down. If they were working hard to give me great opportunities, I wasn't going to take that for granted.

I would pursue cross-country through the end of my schooling. I'd be the best runner that I possibly could be, and every year I would make it all the way to Nationals (as far as you can go in Australia). But from there, I wasn't sure where to go. A lot of my costs had been offset by my parents during high school (which was *very* expensive), but graduation meant any financial help would be gone. They would pay for college itself, but everything else would be on my dime. I couldn't cover the expense that goes into running competition, so after talking to my parents, I decided to retire my running shoes to the back of my closet and enrolled at the Queensland University of Technology in 2011. Originally, I thought about being a vet because I love animals, but I didn't think my grades were good enough to get into veterinary school; I then thought about becoming a midwife or a paramedic, but I had missed out on signing up for specific courses by then and had to choose my third option, so I took nursing and exercise and movement science, with the plan of getting a master's after I graduated.

Starting college meant redirecting my focus from running to my studies. I would exercise, but just exercising for the sake of keeping fit wasn't enough for me. I missed competing. Before university, everything always had a purpose; I'd always been training for this or that competition, so when I didn't have something to train for, I didn't train. Period. I felt I'd lost a big part of my sense of purpose (my why). Being away from my family and Shane, the feeling of loneliness kicked in, and without the running to keep it at bay, I found myself feeling the lowest I'd ever felt in my life. I wanted to get back into running, but I felt I couldn't do both, so I created excuses: "Sports doesn't pay the bills" was a recurring thought. I hadn't seriously trained in a long time, and I thought it would be too hard to get remotely close to my old form. I felt like that ship had sailed and I was too old to go any further. So I stopped participating in all my sports; I stopped everything so that I could focus on my studies. But I soon began to feel that I lost a big part of me; training had been such a huge part of my life, so when I took that out, I literally felt lost.

You would think I would pour my restlessness into my studies, but I had no motivation there. I felt like a complete failure. I started questioning everything. I questioned what I was supposed to do. Was I supposed to finish school and get a job, like everyone else? In what? I rationalized my choice at that point: *Okay, this is what I have to do. Just buckle up.* They would never admit it, but I know deep down my parents worried about me, which made this time all the more upsetting. I wasn't putting in the work and I felt like I was wasting my mum and dad's money. I was disappointed in myself, but I also felt off-kilter. For so long I had identified myself as an athlete, and with that no longer in focus, I doubted who I was and where I was going.

I felt like I was letting my parents down. I always wanted to make them proud, yet here I was just living life and going day by day aimlessly, and not living up to my full potential. I started making unhealthy choices for myself, like eating chocolate for breakfast (seriously), staying up late, sleeping in, and missing my lectures. I know I am not alone in this untethered feeling, this loss of identity; maybe you can relate, but the struggle is real.

Not knowing what I wanted to do, I eventually left school and moved to the coastal town of Gladstone, about six hours' drive north of Brisbane, with Shane, who had landed a job with a mining company. Needless to say, this step did indeed make my parents worry. They wanted me to continue with my education so I could have a career to fall back on, but I just needed a pause to figure out what I wanted. I took a dental-assisting job, then, a bit later, a laboratory-technician position with the company where Shane worked. It was a nice, simple life—I was earning money and felt I was contributing to my future with Shane. It also gave me time to think about my next move. Eventually, running found a way back to me, and I started working out at a local athletic club and competing in races on the weekends. I was training again, and I began to feel like my life was beginning to get back on track. In 2013, Shane, who was playing rugby at the time, had begun his preseason training at the local CrossFit gym. He told me that he thought Cross-Fit could help me with my conditioning for my running, especially its plyometrics and strength workouts.

I went to the gym with Shane a couple days later. I found the workout intriguing, but I had a hard time connecting with the coach; I felt he doubted my abilities as soon as I walked in the door. I didn't expect him to give me any special treatment, but when I asked questions, he looked at me as if I had zero chance of successfully executing any of the movements. Not a good sign, I thought.

Shane encouraged me to give it another shot, and, sure enough, once I got into it, it didn't take me long to become obsessed. It helped me feel more in control of my life and figure out what it was I was truly passionate about. I never thought that running or any sort of fitness plan would be the significant piece I was missing, but as I brought it back into my life, I wished I had cinched up those laces earlier. What I found in

CrossFit was that it felt like *the* ultimate test. It encapsulated all sorts of fitness goals: You have to be strong, powerful, and quick, but you also have to have endurance, a strong skill set, and the ability to adapt to anything. It's like a conglomeration of so many different sports all rolled into one. It would eventually win out over running.

Looking back at this, I realized I had to go through all this uncertainty to get to my why. I am a strong believer that everything happens for a reason. Great things often take time. Anyone who knows me knows that I tend to be impatient, but I am not hasty when it comes to goal setting. Patience and discipline are necessary ingredients for success. So, as you strive toward your goal—it might be the next day, or the next week, or the next month—you may find other sources of motivation. We all evolve and so do our needs; we have to be open-minded to where to find that motivation. For example, I was only going to compete in the 2015 CrossFit Games to set me up for success to qualify for the 2016 Olympics in weight lifting. One Cross-Fit Games turned into eight, because over those years, Shane and I realized that I could try as long as I physically could keep working at this. I could try my hardest to capitalize on this period of my life, work hard now, and reap the rewards later.

It helps to have an end goal. Once you have figured that out, ask yourself: What do I need to do in order to achieve that? So I don't get overwhelmed, I try to simplify it by breaking it down into manageable mini-goals. So, what does that look like? Say I wanted to build my personal record (PR) of a squat to 400 pounds and my starting point is 300 pounds. So, in order to develop 100 pounds, I mapped out a schedule where I would do 310, then build up to 320, etc. It might take four weeks or four years, but that's okay, because I'm chipping away nice and slowly and working consistently toward that end goal.

HOW TO KEEP UP THE MOMENTUM

Tennis is a sport we all watched as a family—much like how everyone watches football in the States. So one of the first athletes who came across my radar as a child was Lleyton Hewitt, one of Australia's top-ranked tennis players. Known as a scrappy player, he won the singles titles at the US Open in 2001 and then Wimbledon in 2002, becoming the youngest men's player ever to earn the number one ranking. Hewitt, among other athletes, mapped out what motivation looks like to me. He inspired me, but I also lived for the adrenaline rush that ran through my veins every time I competed. That passion kept up my momentum.

And keeping the momentum in any practice is key to success. Otherwise, excuses start to creep in, and you will find it harder to go for that run, walk through those gym doors, or start that new diet program. How to keep your mojo?

Find inspiration from others. It may be a simple quote from a book I read or from another athlete, but I'll memorize it and repeat it whenever I need a jolt.

Mix it up. Whatever your skill level, any sort of fitness program can benefit from conditioning. When I first started out with running, my dad knew that swimming would be great for my lung expansion, which would, in turn, help my running. So, we would change it up, adding low-impact work on the body to keep it healthy and avoid injury or overuse. Try to figure out the happy balance between working on endurance and strength as well as agility.

Make it fun. If you watch any of my Instagram feeds, you know I sometimes make my workout sessions a game—especially with Shane. I try to beat him on the barbells or box squats. (I always do, but he never lets me get off easy. He's trying his hardest, too!)

Love the grind. So much of training is about repetition. Jump rope. Do those squats and box jumps. Repeat. Day in, day out. Learn to love the process, meaning that no matter what it takes, embrace each moment and accept every challenge so you can enjoy the journey. It's crucial to *love* the grind.

Train with a buddy. I have found that training with another person is a huge plus for me. Throughout my career I have had the privilege of training alongside other Games athletes, and, believe me when I say, it is pretty motivating having someone likeminded and equally passionate next to me on the rower, *trying* to outpace me.

Intrinsic and Extrinsic Motivation

There is a ton of research on motivation, specifically relating to intrinsic and extrinsic motivation. Extrinsic motivation is about having someone else set your goals for you. Intrinsic motivation is what sort of goals you give yourself. Growing up, I always had that intrinsic motivation, like an alarm clock that jump-started my body every morning. That kind of motivation contributes to your becoming unstoppable. It's that everyday mental GO button that gets you to the gym, to the track, to the pool, so you train the house down, no matter what exercise you're doing. This holds true for getting your ass in the boardroom or classroom as well. The motivation that drives you to put in consistent time and effort in pursuing any goal will get you where you want to go. I struggled with this at college because my motivation was tied to succeeding for other people, not for myself. Moral of the story: I didn't go to college for what I wanted to do, which made it hard to find the motivation to pursue the right career path. I had to learn the hard way that I was wasting my time and money.

Sometimes intrinsic motivation is not enough. That is when extrinsic motivation can spur you on as well. For me, wanting to make Shane and my family proud is a key motivational factor. Because I knew how hard my parents worked to see my dreams come true, I just couldn't let them down. And knowing that Shane has dedicated his life to ensuring my success is not something I take lightly, either.

For Shane's part, he always has been so passionate about fitness, too, but he worked in the mines because that's what everyone told him to do. It was a means to an end. It paid the bills. You always could tell that his heart was somewhere else. He was never satisfied; there was just never that motivation for him. Once we figured out that he could train me and make a name for himself as a coach, all of a sudden, we both had the same motivation—to get me on the CrossFit circuit full-time. No way would we have gotten as far if we hadn't both been fully motivated, locked and loaded.

By the way, this is where I have seen the biggest fracture between the Australian and the US mentality. When I first competed in the United States, I was struck by the difference in extrinsic motivations. I didn't compete to win. Like a typical Australian, I competed to be present, to enjoy the game and the roaring crowd, to meet competitors, and to take in the entire experience. I participated because I loved the act of competition. Winning, of course, is always welcome, but I noticed how some US athletes seem solely focused on that—the win. That is far from the heart of the game. I will say that, having been in America for so long, that winning attitude sometimes takes hold of me, but I notice that the moment I get caught up in being number one, I tense up, and therefore lose my focus. To compete at my best, I need to *let go* of that type of transactional motivation.

SURROUND YOURSELF WITH GOOD PEOPLE

Motivation is contagious—surround yourself with others who cultivate and promote performance. We'll talk more about teamwork in chapter 5, but being with like-minded people can help you on your journey to success, because they simply get it. You'll never need to justify your actions. While CrossFit is an individual sport, I get a lot of motivation out of other athletes, and vice versa. That is the very reason we started our online fitness platform, PRVN Fitness, to begin with—Shane saw how so many of us could encourage and empower each other by working side by side. Friendly competition, sportsmanship, and camaraderie raise the trainings to a whole different level. When I first started out, I kept my circle very small; I didn't want to be disappointed in others' actions or efforts. I always wanted to think that I was invincible, that I could do anything myself. I also had a hard time sharing my thoughts on training because I didn't want to give anything away. But I eventually realized that opening up and allowing people into my life created an extrinsic motivation in me. And, better yet, I motivated others. This group atmosphere creates excellence on all levels, and, besides, you'll undoubtedly have more fun. It is a symbiotic relationship benefiting all parties.

Reevaluate Every Year

I don't want you to think that I'm dialed in every day. Believe me, there are plenty of moments when I find my motivation absent, but as long as I can access my why, I can recharge. And

Shane is always there to help with that, so I can bounce back. My why remains having a family and having time to focus on them. So that's the endgame. It means working toward a future where we have the financial independence so I can be a stay-at-home mum or Shane can be a stay-at-home dad. That's definitely been the reason why I have been working literally every single minute of the day and winning so many CrossFit Games, because it's only going to make me better for my kids.

Motivation can also change from year to year as you change from year to year. Every December Shane and I have a sit-down. We talk about our whys and how I can keep getting better. *What's the reason I'm going to work hard this year? What do I want to achieve? What do we want to do differently?* With vision and focus, we create a game plan to get us there.

Kenyan athlete Eliud Kipchoge, often considered the greatest marathon runner of all time, had a pretty simple why: Like most schoolchildren in Kenya, he started long-distance runs early in life, often running to and from school every day. "You don't know you are running because it is a must," Kipchoge once said. A pretty simple why, but also very profound, don't you think? What is your why?

DON'T GET BURNOUT

If you feel drained, acknowledge it. Don't worry: It happens to the best of us, but address it before you burn out.

Give yourself time, but not too much. Are you engaged in a difficult project at work that is derailing you? Okay, but give yourself a deadline to get back to it.

Reevaluate. Consult your workout buddy or your sources of inspiration. Ask questions. Does anything in your life need recalibrating?

Go back to your why. Has your reason for training changed? Is your purpose self-serving or does it involve a bigger purpose?

CHAPTER 2

Good, Old-Fashioned Hard Yakka

Success Rewards Hard Work and Those Who Dare

My dad was a plumber and roofer by trade, but those jobs would only fill in the time when he wasn't working on the farm. Farm life comes with many responsibilities, and before I could go off and explore, there was always hard yakka to be done. *Hard yakka* is Aborigine for "hard work," especially manual labor. Queensland's lush soil is perfect for sugarcane, so my family and surrounding neighbors lived and breathed by the crop's seasons. "Sugarcane doesn't harvest itself," my dad liked to say, as I sat alongside him on the tractor wheel cover as he plowed the fields. It was physically demanding work with little downtime, as the sugarcane process is long and there was always so much to do.

For much of my childhood I was too young to help my dad and grandfather cut the cane by hand, haul it all onto the trailer, and go out to the fields to plant the roots into the ground, but watching my parents work so hard day in and day out shaped me. As hard as they chugged away, with their calloused hands and their skin weathered from the sun, there was a quiet dignity in all they did; I knew that no matter what I was going to be when I got older, I would do it with the same commitment.

Perhaps that's why, when I started running, it didn't seem like a big deal for me to get up at 5 a.m. to train. My mum was usually already up with my two younger sisters, Elle, seven years younger than me, and Molly, ten years younger. In fact, it was right around the time that Molly was born that my favorite sports teacher, Gwyn, encouraged me to do cross-country. I had shown some ability, I was willing to work, and he wanted to see how far I could go. My dad became my coach—on top of everything else!—and with measuring tape and some handy spray paint, we marked 400, 800, and 1,500 meters into the perimeter of our property's headland so I had a homemade track I could train on. There I'd practice as my dad worked; it really helped me in the wintertime to know that he was already out on the fields on his tractor, with its lights visible in the distance. If he could be out there in the frigid blackness of early morning, I could, too. I knew he already had his smoko—a morning break for tea. With one more quick break for lunch, he'd be back in the fields until dark, making it a 15-hour workday.

Talent versus Hard Work

This work ethic was ingrained in me, and it informs how I train today and how I approach anything in life. Having talent is one thing, what you *do* with that talent is another, and I grew up learning that responsibility for yourself is key, and you can't just sit back and wait for things to happen. There is a phrase we'd say all the time back home—*"All yak and no yakka"*—to describe someone who's all talk and no action. These folks are more interested in sounding important than in *doing* something important. I see this play out all the time in the world of competing.

Much as sugarcane needs to be constantly nurtured and fed, our talents and abilities need to be nurtured. So, talent alone won't ensure success—it only happens when you put in the effort. This is especially true in CrossFit, since the sport draws from so many individual movements. Someone can be a naturally fast runner, but speed is only needed for part of the competition, as there will be events that call for endurance and other fitness components, like skill, strength, and power. That's why it's great to see so many diverse athletes in the Games—those who make it there succeeded in pushing themselves where they don't have natural abilities in order for them to excel in the sport. They learned to lean on what I consider another essential talent—discipline. It is indeed a talent to show up day after day, focused and ready to work hard. Talent is what gets your foot in the door. But, boy, for you to get *through* that door, you've got to actually put in the work. Sure, people may think I have attributes that are beyond those of the average person, but it really comes down to my work ethic superseding my talent.

No excuses, no shortcuts. Do you put your head down and push through anything, or are you all about showing off how much you can dead-lift, posting it on Instagram for all the instant likes? Do you think your talents alone are going to get you where you want to go? Because if you do, you've got another thing coming.

Nothing Comes Easy

I hate excuses, but I hate shortcuts more. I've never taken them and never will. They are both cop-outs. There was never a day that I did not give it my best. Even if you come up short, you win the day knowing you gave it your all. As the late and great NBA basketball star Bill Russell famously said, "If a guy pays you $5, give him $7 worth of work."

When I was 12 and training for Nationals, it was about a week before the race, and I was excited about it. "Oh, my God, this is the year, isn't it? This is gonna be the year I win. I have trained the house down and given it my honest best. Every. Single. Day." Wouldn't you know it, a few days later, I got really, really sick. It wasn't contagious, but I could feel how much it was affecting my energy. We had already traveled 16 hours to Townsville, the town where the race was being held, and my dad told me, "You know, you don't have to do this." But I was adamant. I competed the best I could and placed 10th. No one had a clue I was sick as a dog, and that was okay with me. I showed up and gave it my all.

Fast-forward 15 years to the 2022 CrossFit games. An old back injury came back with a vengeance a few weeks before the first day of competition. My entire family had already flown in to be with me in Madison, Wisconsin, and we all had serious conversations about whether I could compete at all. It was two weeks from the Games, and I couldn't even get out of bed. The question of whether I could compete at all was on everyone's mind. Even as I struggled—I tried all our go-to recovery remedies, from anti-inflammatory foods and massages to ice baths—I was not about to give up. While I worried that I wouldn't be in the right physical condition to compete, I would never let my competitors know that anything was wrong and let them smell blood. I was not going to allow this setback to become an excuse.

I often meet people who are quick to throw up roadblocks to their success. They'll say things like, "I can't do that because I have an old back injury . . ." or "That sport is just *so* expensive" or "I just don't have the time to train because my job is just so all-consuming." True, our lives are filled with responsibilities, deadlines, and just dealing with life's daily grind. But, if you look at people who have made it work, you'll see across the board that they have accepted the challenges of money, time, and effort and thought creatively about how to fit those challenges into their lifestyle. If money is an issue, there are so many things you can do for free—take up running, do an online workout, lift weights at home. If it is time, think of places where you can squeeze in a workout, whether it's early in the day, during lunch, or after work. If motivation is lacking, try to find a workout buddy who will get you off your couch. If you really want to do something, you will find a way—no excuses.

HARD WORK...IS HARD WORK

If you need some help getting started, here are some tips that help me stay on track:

1. **Schedule it.** Put it in your calendar. Lock in the day and time, and block out a certain amount of time to do it.

2. **Leave cues.** If you need to exercise, lay your workout clothes on the back of your bedroom chair or put your sneakers right by your front door. Maybe you put an inspirational quote on a sticky note and place it on your bathroom mirror. (I write mine in red lipstick on my bathroom mirror so I can see it every day: WIN THE CROSSFIT GAMES.) If you need an extra push to even get up early in the morning, program your coffee to be made on a timer. Nothing beats the smell of coffee to get you out of bed.

3. **Show up.** Most of the time, just showing up is the hardest part. The fact that you did just that shows great promise. Now follow through. Once I get my game on— within 10 minutes or so—I forget about all the hemming and hawing to get myself there.

4. **Trick your brain.** James Clear, in his book *Atomic Habits*, talks about how motivation kicks in *after* you start

doing something you have been putting off. Give your-self those first 10 minutes to get your endorphins to kick in; it gets easier after that. Before you know it, an hour has gone by, and you will feel so much better for it.

5. **Give yourself a break.** I always have a rest day; give yourself one, too. It's crucial to have balance in your life. If you find yourself skipping a day here and there and slipping back into bad habits, get back on track as soon as possible. If you don't have time for an hour-long work-out, do 20 minutes instead. At least you did something. Consistency is essential. Just level it up the next time. Also, don't overcomplicate things—when things become overwhelming, you can start to feel defeated.

6. **Set daily goals.** I have a whiteboard calendar at home where I write down five goals for the day every morning, and, in the evening, I take a look to see if I "won" or "lost" that day. A typical list for me would be: Read, drink 64 ounces of water, meditate, mobilize, learn something new. I would have to do all five in order for me to label it a win, so either there would be a big "W" marked in blue in the day's box or a large "L" in red for that day so I could easily see how I did. Hopefully, by the end of the week I would have seven blue Ws, but I wouldn't beat myself up if I had ended up with an L or two.

7. **Reward yourself.** With that same calendar, see how long you can continue the Ws on days that you make prog-ress. Give yourself milestones—maybe it is a week's worth of Ws—in which you reward yourself with a nice meal or a trip to the movies. I often set date nights with Shane as my reward. It helps in those times I want to slack off, and I remind myself what I'd miss out on if I did!

Train with Purpose and Intention

Some people go to the gym to release steam, others go for me time, and still others go for fun. If you are happy exercising to keep fit or de-stress, great, but if you are reading this book, you are probably very driven and looking for that edge in competition. So here is why I go: I am working on what Shane and I call "purposeful training." I train with a goal in mind and everything I do in and outside of the gym is geared toward that goal. I am trying to be better than I was yesterday (so I can later wipe any competition off the floor). And tomorrow, I am going to be better than I was today (so I am unbeatable). While I physically exert a lot of energy, I also push myself mentally. Every bike or rowing session has a purpose behind it. And I remind myself that *If I don't push hard here, then that could be the difference between me winning or losing.* It is mentally draining and undeniably physically painful, but it is worth it to ensure that I am standing on top of the podium at the end of the season. Am I shaving off a second on that row pace? Did I lift 10–15 more pounds that will make all the difference in the next competition?

Everything has intention—even everything I do outside the gym. What I do in my free time is just as important. For instance, when I'm home, rather than sitting on the couch watching TV, I'll stretch while catching up on my favorite shows. Shane always says, "Don't be just focused on what you do in the hour you spend in the gym, but also be focused on what you do during the other 23 hours outside of the gym." It's important for me to know where I'm going and identify everything I need to do to achieve that goal. If I am aware of that intention, I buy into it a lot more, particularly when I am in the trenches, and it feels like Groundhog Day every day, just executing movement after movement. These moments are exactly when I need to remember why we're doing all this.

Some people say to themselves, "I ran three miles. I did my exercise for the day . . ." Nope, you are not done. And for others who say, "I love training, I can do it all day," I say to you that you must not be pushing yourself hard enough because you should hurt so much that you curse it and it is nearly impossible for you to go on. That is where the important distinction lies between exercise and training: People think they train on a regular basis, but really, they are just exercising. Exercise doesn't have a training plan or structure; it is for the casual fitness enthusiast, who is exercising for overall health, to clear the head, or to give themselves me time. Training is done with purpose.

If you truly want to get better, stronger, perhaps even compete, you'll need to integrate purposeful training into your workouts. It's more than just keeping track of the time displayed on your treadmill touchscreen. If you push yourself that hard and truly go to your limit, you wouldn't enjoy it—you would hate it as I do—but you'd do it to get to the next level. The feeling of showcasing your true potential in front of a crowd on the world stage far outweighs the pain I feel every day in the gym. When people say they train hard, I would challenge them and ask, "But are you doing so with purpose?" (P.S.: No one in the world trains harder than me!)

TRACKING OUR TRAINING

When I am in full training mode, I am working at it for roughly 8–10 hours a day. When we first start the season, I don't go out the gate that intensely. I start with about 2 hours' worth of work, and at the back end of that are a lot of recovery protocols. As the season progresses, we start adding more time and adding more sessions and pieces to our training. I will go up to 2–3 hours and then to 3–4 hours and then to 5–6. For instance, I'll do a warm-up and workout at 8 a.m. Then there will be a rest, and, after that, I'll do another workout at 10:30 a.m, then another one from 1 to 2: 30 p.m., getting in four to five workouts in a day. And then when we're weeks out from the Games we go up from 6 to 8 to 10 hours—that time block is to mirror the CrossFit Games. It's what we call "progression overload," but it's implemented over time so my body can adapt to it. We make sure to track recovery along the way: Shane uses a numbers-based rating system of 1–10; sometimes it can go to 11 if it is extremely hard. A chart would look like this:

1–2 Easy-peasy 😊

3–4 Easy and enjoyable

5–6 Puffing a bit

7–8 Challenging but still doable

9–10 Having trouble continuing

11 Can't go on

If at the end of the session, I tell him I am at a 3 or 4, he knows he needs to push me harder. If I give him a 9 or a 10, then he knows I am due for a rest, and he may try to figure out if there is anything going on that is tiring me out. The next day, we may reduce my training blocks so that if I feel like a 7 or 8 by the end of the workout, we know that I am recovering better than the previous day.

The key here is for you to have *a measured and intentional* training; hours of mindlessly and idly doing something is not going to do much for you. The idea is this: You train with purpose, understand what you want to achieve, understand what that looks like, and you do that so many times that it becomes second nature. Everything should have an intention—and you should always be aware of it. Ask yourself every day, every month: What is the purpose here? What am I trying to achieve? Does this align with my goals? And always come up with an answer. If you don't, search for it. Mine is always changing. In 2014, I was focused on getting to the Olympics. In 2023, it was eating healthily for two!

I see people fall into this trap all the time when they're training for competition. They think that as long as they are hurting, they're doing everything they can to win. Not true. Not every single workout has to be gut-wrenchingly hard—but every single workout should be done with purpose and intention. And that means respecting the sport and following the rules that you'll come up against in competition. This includes practicing good form or timing—for example, stepping over the line before the buzzer is a no-no. Now, of course, I have made false starts before. I am not perfect; accidents do happen. But it happens more to athletes who don't practice with intention. They get penalized, they walk off the floor, flabbergasted. One year an athlete stepped on a line and was removed from competition, and he thought that the judges were in the wrong. He'll never get on the podium if he doesn't realize that the devil is in the details, and those small things are just a reflection of how we deal not only with competing but with bigger issues in life as well.

Mistakes Were Made

In my years hanging out at the gym, I have seen all sorts of people make mistakes—rookies and long-timers alike. Heck, I can still get caught up in one or two of these. Here is what you should avoid if you are an aspiring elite athlete.

Rookie Mistakes

When I first started out, I made a few of these, I cannot tell a lie!

1. Training too hard or too heavy too soon. As a newbie, I was impatient and wanted to learn everything

yesterday, and, at first, I didn't appreciate the time it took to improve.

2. Not being consistent. Especially when you're first starting out, you need to be in the gym four to five days a week consistently so you can develop a healthy, deliberate practice.

3. Not eating right. You read about my chocolate cravings earlier, as well as my not-so-healthy diet. What you eat can affect a workout and your performance, so, early on, find a good nutrition plan that works for you.

4. Buying too much equipment. After just the first few weeks of getting into the sport, I bought everything and anything I could. (I told you I am impatient!) I know now this was not necessary. You don't need every gadget and the latest sneakers to do CrossFit properly. Ease into it, and see what works for you and what you need as opposed to what you *think* you need.

Veteran Mistakes

1. Overtraining and not valuing your recovery.
2. Getting caught up in rankings, and your competitors' rankings, instead of focusing on the fundamentals of basic training.
3. Not focusing on your own weaknesses. I am naturally strong, but I had to work on weight lifting because I

needed to get better at it. Work on your weak spots to improve; don't ignore them.

4. Small changes lead to big change. Detail is important.
5. Getting distracted by the hype (believing your own press) and forgetting your goals. Some athletes get caught up in honing their own image, and that can lead to self-esteem problems. Because they are the first to be scrutinized, they lose sight of their performance and devote more energy to their appearance.

Angela Duckworth, in her best-selling book *Grit*, spotlights a theory by sociologist Dan Chambliss about the "mundanity of excellence." Those small, seemingly "mundane" things that you do, day in and day out, will eventually enable you to excel at something. Whether it is writing, performing, or playing a sport, there really is no shortcut to success. Everything takes time and patience. (In her TED Talk on grit, she describes it as "sticking with your future, day in, day out, not just for the week, not just for the month, but for years, and working really hard to make that future a reality. Grit is living life like it's a marathon, not a sprint.")

ARE YOU GIVING IT YOUR ALL?

Talk is cheap. Everyone thinks they work hard. But the way I see it, there is always more to do; sometimes people just don't recognize it. They think they are doing everything possible to achieve a goal, but they aren't all-in because they don't believe in themselves 100 percent. Some people think they are doing their absolute best, but something may be holding them back, whether that is a fear of succeeding or a fear of putting themselves out there fully. They have ready explanations to fall back on when they fail: "I didn't win because I had an injury" or "I didn't win because I didn't have the right team." Do you find yourself giving the same excuses? Looking back on the last 24 hours, ask yourself this question: Do you think you are doing enough?

> Are you using your free time (outside work hours) wisely? (Did you go out too late instead of staying in and getting a good night's sleep?)

> What distractions can you cut out of your daily life? (Quick answer: Stop scrolling!)

> How can you better organize your time outside the gym to maximize your time in the gym? For instance, can you do weekly meal preps to save time on cooking?

> Are you maintaining a healthy routine? I hear so many people complain about poor posture because of their daily job. Can you spare 10–20 minutes a day to stretch or mobilize your body?

How did you answer these? Did you identify areas where you could improve?

Trust in the Process

I put enormous trust in my process because it gives me the ability to be prepared no matter what. Because I've built a foolproof foundation, I've trained myself to adapt, allowing me to perform at my best under any circumstances.

Here's an example: The first time I went to the CrossFit Games, in 2015, I was just excited to be there. But I also came to conquer. With the nature of CrossFit, you never know what curveball you will be thrown because you never know the Games' program until hours before competition. Since no one ever knows what specific events will be chosen until a few days before or even the day before, you have to be prepared for anything and everything. When the events were finally announced, Shane and I were reviewing the program when both of us stopped dead on "Pegboard." I didn't know what a pegboard was. My first time doing it would be out on the competition floor in front of tens of thousands of people.

I shot a look to Shane.

"Do you think I can do this?" I mumbled. I could feel myself tense up. *Oh, crap, maybe I am not ready,* I thought. I had the advantage of rookie luck: No one expected me to perform well, but I still had my own expectations to live up to.

"Okay, maybe you haven't done this exact movement, but you have done ones like this. You've done pull-ups, you've done rope climbs. All you have to do is not panic and just stay focused. I can guarantee you'll be able to climb up that pegboard," Shane replied.

I was calmed by Shane's words, and I also reminded myself that the nervousness I was feeling actually stemmed from the excitement of doing something new.

I forgot about the competitors to my left and right and just focused on one peg at a time. I didn't rush, I didn't panic, and I didn't allow myself to get overwhelmed. Because at the end of the day, I knew I had done the work.

When you show up, put in the work, and you trust it, then you can truly achieve. I went to bed that night knowing I had done my best.

Like everyone else, when I first started CrossFit, I was far behind all the other competitors, but because of that deliberate practice I was committed to, I've been able to accomplish in a short time what others have taken years to achieve. It is not just the time you put in. Countless hours of working out mindlessly won't do much for you. Endless hours of determination and focus will. I have seen plenty of athletes who had started much earlier than I did, but I managed to catch up—and surpass them. All because I trusted the process.

Suffer Now . . .

Don't get me wrong, I hate training. *Hate* it. But I know what I am after—the top podium—and that keeps me going. I do the work because I know what could be mine. I take comfort in knowing I am not alone. Muhammad Ali once said, "I hated every minute of training, but I said, 'Don't quit. Suffer now and live the rest of your life as a champion.'" Hard work is where you build consistency, and all that time and deliberate effort will show up in your performance. That's your endgame. You want to train so consistently that everything and anything you do—maintaining your posture in your clean and jerks, breathing with precise timing during your GHD sit-ups, knowing you're hitting rowing paces without looking at the monitor—becomes second nature. The movements and actions will feel so natural that when you do go out onto that competition floor (or into that boardroom, onto that stage, or into that classroom), your instincts will take over and you will run like a machine. If you have done something 10, 100, even 1,000 times, something that felt incredibly hard at first will start to feel easier and easier, until the move feels like you were born to do it. You probably have heard about the 10,000-hour rule, made famous by Malcolm Gladwell (and based on research by psychologist Anders Ericsson). The amount is a bit arbitrary—10,000 is just a catchy and provocative number (but also a fun one to keep as a goal)—but the idea behind the theory has become bedrock for Shane and me. The premise is true: It does take thousands of hours to truly master something. In 2021, I finally hit that 10,000-hour rule for CrossFit, the same year Shane hit his mark, too, because he's coached for me and others for more than 10,000 hours. Even though I hate training, I do the suffering now so I, too, can live the rest of my life knowing I did it to get to where I am.

1 Percent Changes

Shane likes to talk about the 1 percent rule—the concept that a series of small, incremental steps will lead to big changes over a certain amount of time. Maybe a 1 percent change in one area of your life may not make or break any records, but when you combine that 1 percent change with another 1 percent change, it can create a compound effect. You will be so encouraged that you will be trying to make 1 percent changes in every area of your life. You may feel that something may take forever to achieve, but if you attack each small goal with enthusiasm and passion, you will see how quickly those small achievements add up to big change. By making 1 percent changes that become good habits, you will become the best version of yourself. Take a look at my daily schedule—it is built out of mini-habits. Every day, I get up early to train—something I started doing when I began running competitively. I wake up, have a glass of water, enjoy a cup of coffee with a good self-help book, then I go on to meditate while I'm stretching. I check emails, then I start training. I am aware that what I do outside of the gym helps contribute to making me a champion on the competition floor. Having a productive regimen that you stick to is a key component of success. When I don't have that routine, I get a little lost and lose my focus.

This idea bleeds into another concept: How you do one thing is how you should do everything. We are talking as granular as how you put your dumbbells away or how you leave your station—is it clean for the next person to use? And, closer to home, how do you leave your kitchen sink? I am telling you that if that kitchen sink is constantly filled with dishes, I'll bet other parts of your life are pretty messy, too. It can feel tedious and time-consuming to focus on the little details, but those all add up and help contribute to—or detract from—your performance (and your life). It's easy for people to get distracted or bored when doing this—I get that—but attention to detail is important.

For example, if I have to wash dishes, I make sure I wash those darn dishes well. When I fold clothes, they are folded in a way that would make Marie Kondo proud. When I go to the gym, I always leave it cleaner than when I walked in. Clean house, clean life. Always do things with the highest level of professionalism, and creating good habits helps you do that. If you cop out in training or make excuses for how you do—or don't do—the smallest of tasks, excuses will bleed into other parts of your life.

Contrary to the popular myth that it takes 21 days for a new habit to form, studies show that it actually takes more like two months or more to develop a new habit. So, you have to stick to whatever you want to make a habit—don't overload yourself; make one change at a time. Being overly ambitious will actually set you up for failure—one false move and you'll feel defeated. Once you successfully create one habit, try adding another. And then another. For example: Making sure you stretch before a workout, giving your body a rest day once a week, drinking more water—these are all good, manageable habits that add up to a great fitness plan. No matter how seemingly small they are, these types of incremental changes win the day over time. When it comes to habit-making, even if you improve a little bit over a week, month, or year, you will eventually become exponentially better at whatever it is you do.

Sidenote: One habit I am trying to work on is being more chill in training, because I know I can be super intense and I have incredibly high (some would say impossible) expectations. But as my team members can attest, I fall short at times. They appreciate my efforts, though, and laugh at me whenever I get too fiery. I keep on trying.

Believe me, I still have moments when my nerves get to me, but whenever they start, I think of this line from Shane: "Keep it simple, T. Find your flow, let your body do its thing." And with that, I can breathe.

So, I have learned to embrace my nerves hanging out in my stomach. It means I care and I am still hungry for competition. I am not the only one who can appreciate this. Formula 1 race car driver and fellow Aussie Daniel Ricciardo has said, "Enjoy the butterflies. Enjoy the nerves. The pressure. People not knowing your name, all that stuff. Enjoy the process of making the name for yourself."

ESSENTIAL GEAR FOR YOUR GRIND

When I first started CrossFit, I was adamant that if I wasn't bleeding, bruised, or battered, then I was not working hard enough. But, in time, I realized that my body being banged up wasn't great for the next day's training and the day after that. So I smartened up and started thinking about what was best for my body. Here's a list of what I consider essential training gear. I use these every day and they come with me everywhere I go, even when I'm on the road. These will help you up your game as well as keep you comfortable and prevent injury.

Barbell. You want good-quality equipment, so look for a barbell that spins well. If it doesn't, it can hinder the way you perform the movement.

Clock. CrossFit is all about racing against time, so having a small clock to keep track of time is very handy. I like to take this with me as I move around the gym to different equipment. Make sure yours has a long battery life.

Hand grips (or gymnastic grips). Many of us CrossFitters use gymnastic grips to protect our hands when performing pull-ups or other gymnastic movements. Look for ones that are light and sturdy so they help when gripping on the bar, especially when it comes to toe to bar, muscle-ups, and chest or pull-ups.

Elbow and knee sleeves. These compression sleeves are great for the joints, so I use these if I have a bit of a sore elbow or knee and need some extra support. They also ease pain, improve blood flow, and promote muscle recovery.

Foam roller. Ah, I love these before and after a workout. Not only do they help massage the tightness out of your muscles, they help increase circulation, warm up the muscles, and reduce muscle soreness. You can use them any-time, anywhere that you feel a tightness or pain to ease the discomfort.

Speed rope. A speed rope is a staple in my daily routine. When purchasing one, make sure you get the fastest rope, which will help you on the competition floor, and that means they should be super light, with smooth handles that rotate easily.

Resistance band. This is another staple in my daily routine—it's great for stretching, especially for the upper body. It has to have the right amount of tension in it to give me a really nice stretch throughout the shoulders. I typically stretch early in the morning when I first wake up, but that's when I do more static stretches. Later, when I'm at the gym, I do more dynamic stretches—and utilize these bands—to get my blood flowing and my body warmed up.

Thumb tape. When I'm doing a lot of hand workouts, like hand cleans and snatches, this comes in handy (no pun intended) to protect my thumb and fingers. Get a brand that is not too rigid—you want your thumbs to be able to bend easily. Remember: Don't use too much—too much pressure on the thumb can bruise it.

Training shoes. I have three pairs with me at all times: Runners for, um, running; lifters especially made for weight lifting; and trainers that I wear for everything else. I go through two pairs of lifters every season because I'm always in them and they're just so supportive.

Water. I can't say it enough: Hydration is key, so I always have my water bottle near me. I add salt packets to keep up my hydration levels to ensure that I am never depleted and I can keep going.

Weight-lifting belt. I don't like to be too reliant on a belt, but I will use one when I do heavy squats or some kind of strength cycle. It helps support your back, which helps you lift for longer and keeps you from pulling any muscles.

Lifting straps. When performing heavy clean pulls or snatch pulls, I use these to help build strength and ensure that I am maintaining good technique while lifting a substantial load. This removes the grip component and allows me to just focus on building strength.

Wrist wraps. When I need that wrist support for anything overhead—handstand push-ups or handstand walks—these are my go-to. I like mine thick and super sturdy. They are also good to use when doing a bench press or a clean and jerk, and they offer good stability when doing dumbbells or kettlebells.

Make the Time

It may seem easy for me to say now, but I didn't just wake up and become the most dominant CrossFit athlete of all time. My success has afforded me the ability to train 24/7, but that was not always the case. I never had issues with motivation (Shane will tell you that) because I knew how important that was to achieving my goals. Rather, it was time. When I first started CrossFit, I was working as a lab technician at a mining company that had 12-hour night shifts and day shifts. I would work for two days from 7 a.m. to 7 p.m. and three nights from 7 p.m. to 7 a.m. I'd train for CrossFit during my off-hours. On the day shifts, I would get to the gym around 7:30 p.m., after working the 12-hour shift, do a 2½-hour workout, go home, and do it all over again the next day. On my night shifts, I'd get a workout in before work. If you want to truly do something, you find a way. And while it was challenging and exhausting at times, I could appreciate my progress even more because of all that struggle. I think these hardships—when properly tapped into—can create a phenomenal foundation for future success. We all need to recognize where our roadblocks are and build simple steps to climb over them. I often look back to those early days and think, *If we made it work with those circumstances, we can make anything work.*

Creating a formidable work ethic is the foundation of practically everything we cover in this book. *Hard work is where consistency and good habits are formed. Be patient and trust in this process.* Think of hard work as the hub of a bicycle wheel—the center from which all the spokes (one is passion, another is talent) radiate. Without that hub, you can't go anywhere. With it, nothing can stop you.

CHAPTER 3

Feed the Good Wolf

Embrace Failure and Turn Fear into Fuel

The thick Australian bush that surrounded our family farm was home for all sorts of wildlife, so there wasn't much room for fear to creep in. Once, when I was about seven, I had been reaching for my favorite toy in the living room when I noticed something slithering behind Mr. Potato Head and onto the floor to the right side of me. I screamed for my dad, who came running to see what was wrong.

As soon as he saw our house guest, a carpet snake, he turned to me and said, "You know, Tia, we are actually encroaching on its habitat here, so we need to be respectful. It is not being aggressive to you, so you just have to let it do its thing, and it will go away. Don't be scared—he is probably more frightened of you than you are of him." He was right, the carpet snake was harmless—unlike some of the other wildly dangerous snakes and spiders we have in Australia—and great to have around the farm, as they ate all the rats and mice.

As I grew older, I realized that life was filled with things more scary than snakes, but my parents always encouraged me to face any fear head-on and to do things that pushed my boundaries. When I started running, they didn't let the lack of opportunity around us dampen my enthusiasm—it wasn't as if we had our pick of coaches and facilities to train in, there in the Australian bush, after all. I had to run barefoot sometimes because I didn't have the right shoes, and a proper training facility was about 60 miles away in Brisbane. But rather than be deterred by the lack of options, we made it work. I look back now, amazed at how my parents thought of creative ways to make it happen. Today, while some people may complain about not having the best gear, I see an opportunity to train harder. When I see people throw in the towel because they didn't have the right equipment, I see an opportunity to try something different. I have taken every situation and turned it into a way to get better, just as my dad and mum did with whatever new sport of the week I was into.

Fear of Screwing Up

This is all a buildup to say that I had a comfortable relationship with fear all my life. Because of the scrappy way I grew up, I dealt with whatever was thrown at me with relative ease.

I wasn't fazed by anything I tried. That is, until later, when I began doing CrossFit. By 2014, I had been getting more and more into the sport, with weight lifting a big part of the program. Without any coaching, I could clean and jerk 187 pounds at only 115 pounds in body weight. Great numbers, I was told. But I knew I could do better. And I wanted to do better. At a local competition in Brisbane—my first-ever individual CrossFit competition—a weight-lifting coach named Miles Wydall was there and saw in me a "small, skinny, strong" female who could clean and jerk that heavy and only one of three people to clear the C&J ladder. Renowned for coaching several Olympians, Miles believed I had great potential and wanted to help Shane and me learn our technique and develop my strength. He told me, "You've got hunger and great strength. With more of an understanding of the sport and its technique, who knows where you could go?" He was ready to coach me for the Commonwealth Games—and he even thought I could go as far as the 2016 Rio Olympics. (The Commonwealth Games is a sporting event, much like the Olympics, made up of competitors from mostly former British territories.)

Wydall ran the Cougars Weightlifting Club in Brisbane, so every four weeks Shane and I would drive six hours south to meet with him. It was a long way to go, but the benefit in having him help with my technique and the way I moved up the rankings was well worth the drive. I was faced with a sink-or-swim scenario and I was going to make sure I swam. I decided to quit my lab job and bought my CrossFit gym at the start of 2015, so I could dive all-in on qualifying for the one coveted spot at the 2016 Rio Summer Olympics for the Australian weight-lifting team. It's crazy to think that I left a secure job in the mines at Rio Tinto to own and operate a gym so I could train for the Olympics—a long shot—but we saw it as a risk worth taking.

Around this time, I heard CrossFitter Jason Khalipa say on a podcast that if there's a goal that you want to go out and achieve, you aren't prepared to do it until you actually say it out loud. Boom. That resonated so much with me—it was something I needed to hear right at that time.

One night, Shane and I were closing the gym up after everyone had completed their workouts. We were putting our gym bags in the back of the car, and I turned to Shane and said, "I want to go to the Games." I wanted to see how good I really was—and telling Shane about my new goal put it out in the universe. It became real. I voiced it to him first because I knew he'd help me get there, but once I told him, I let my family and friends know, too. Once I vocalized how badly I wanted to go, that is when the fear kicked in. I suddenly felt the weight of expectations to do the work and make it a reality. No one said anything; it was all me placing that pressure on myself, and I started becoming very scared of failing. My family always had my back in everything I did, so I never wanted them to be disappointed in me. It was a huge motivational factor, but it also caused a panic. If I fell short of my goals, I would be letting down not just myself but them as well. That pressure (which I put on myself) made me tighten up and doubt myself for the first time. I have to admit, it's pretty scary to put yourself out there and hope that you are doing everything you can do to turn your goals and dreams into a reality.

What was going through my head? Well, simply put: *Don't screw this up. Don't be a failure.* This thought, which felt like a big virtual sandbag I had to carry, would bring on a tension that would inevitably trip me up if I let it. I would take a bit longer on a pull-up or lose a fraction of time on a workout. And that second could cost me an event. So, the lesson here: The mere flash of doubt can hold you back. You need to instead remain positive. Easier said than done, I know. But Shane and I worked out a few ways to overcome it. First was flipping the script on this negative thought. When I turn it around and say, "I've got this," it does the same for my body. I relax, and I can focus and do what I came to do rather than focusing on "what if" and coming up short. I call it feeding your good wolf—you need to feed your body positive energy, which allows you to compete at your best.

This good wolf/bad wolf concept actually comes from an anonymous Cherokee parable:

One evening an old Cherokee told his grandson about a battle that goes on inside people.

He said, "My son, the battle is between two wolves inside us all. One is evil. It is anger, envy, jealousy, sorrow, regret, greed, arrogance, self-pity, guilt, resentment, inferiority, lies, false pride, superiority, and ego."

"The other is good. It is joy, peace, love, hope, serenity, humility, kindness, benevolence, empathy, generosity, truth, compassion, and faith."

The grandson thought about it for a minute and then asked his grandfather, "Which wolf wins?"

The old Cherokee simply replied, "The one you feed."

How did we integrate this into my practice? First, I started visualizing myself as a champion rather than a participant (a concept we will get into a little bit later). To help with this, Shane pivoted his coaching and communications to be a consistent voice of positive reinforcement that mirrored my own thoughts. I started to view everything in my life—from the food I ate to the shoes I wore—as making a path leading me toward gold.

This parable also helped me to understand that fear is a perfectly normal human reaction to the unknown. For sure, the amygdala in the brain hijacks that flight-or-fight response to perceived threats. When you fear something, your heart rate goes up, your breathing quickens—that is your body reacting to a threat. What are you going to do with that reaction? Are you going to tighten up from fear? Or are you going to fight? I know which one I'd pick every time.

It helps to know that fear is natural, and every time I step on the floor or field, I need to push through it. It took me a while to fully get to this point, but I now understand that we need to fail, because without failure, we are not pushing ourselves, and without pushing ourselves, we can't get better. But do it on your own terms. Shane always says that failing on someone else's terms only leads to disappointment. If I fail on my own terms, I will be very accepting of that failure. That is so true. Don't get me wrong, I still feel paralyzed at times, but I will think to myself, *If I don't actually try, how am I going to learn? How am I going to evolve?* Once I accepted this, I really started to see results. By embracing fear and allowing myself to fail, I was able to turn negativity into something positive. I started becoming aware of the importance of the process.

Having butterflies is fine—it means you're alive!—but feeling anxious and fearful can exhaust you and make you tense up, make you slower. You are quicker if you are relaxed. Take a page from Bruce Lee: "The less effort, the faster and more powerful you will be."

To be a successful athlete, it is crucial to overcome this fear of failing. If you don't, you're just going to hold yourself back, plain and simple. And you won't get the chance to mentally and physically push yourself to reach your goals. Most importantly, you will never reach that destination nor look back to see the amazing path that you took to get you there. It was because of those defining features throughout that process that I made it to this point. It's okay to fail, because those moments define your story and shape how you overcome all those obstacles.

All this work on fear helped me take on the CrossFit Games in 2015 and land at second place as a rookie, which is practically unheard of. And I immediately thought to myself, *I need to go back again. I need to show myself and the world that it wasn't a fluke.* CrossFit wasn't just about helping me train for the Olympics anymore. I had something to prove. But fear wasn't done with me yet.

Fear of Succeeding

After coming in second in 2015, all I wanted to do was reach the same goal in 2016. It may sound funny now, but when I started doing CrossFit competitively, I never really considered the thought of winning the CrossFit Games because I didn't think I would be doing this sport for that long. When I first started, I didn't think I could afford it long term. It was more of a fun hobby to see what I was capable of. Even after my strong finish in 2015, I still wasn't fully on board with the idea that I could actually take the top spot on the podium. Shane knew at that point that I had trained hard enough and tried to convince me, leading into the 2016 Games, that it was mine to win. But

I remember thinking, *It's just not that easy to win the World Championships. That's on another level. These women have been doing this sport for years. I have only been doing it for five minutes in comparison; it's just not supposed to happen for such a new athlete.* I also couldn't ignore all the naysayers and people who viewed me as a fluke for the past 12 months. It was hard not to think that coming in second was just a lucky break, after all.

But the moment I secured that second-place spot again, I realized I had been too scared to succeed. I had handed first place away by not aiming high enough. I had limited myself by being satisfied with coming in second. I let the outside noise get inside my head. You only get as good as you give, and there was something deep down that was holding me back. I hadn't yet fully embraced the confidence in my own abilities.

I was too careful because I didn't want to make any mistakes. I stopped attacking. I could have won, but I didn't because of that fear of leaping to that next level. I walked off the field knowing I could have done better, and I know Shane could see the disappointment in my face. Standing up on that podium isn't just about me—it is also for my team of people who get me up there. And I let those people down—Shane, my family, my friends. I didn't fight hard enough for them or myself.

DON'T FEAR SUCCESS

Many people are scared to fail, but there are some who can be scared to succeed. They will put up barriers to protect themselves from the horrible feeling of falling short of something, and they believe (irrationally) that they can't reach their goal or fulfill their aspiration. They can't help but get in their own way. And research shows that it's worse for women.

Whether this difference in approach stems from nature or nurture (probably a little of both), women tend to be a bit more hesitant than men when it comes to taking on something new or hard. We overthink and second-guess ourselves to death and tend to underestimate ourselves. Studies have shown that men overestimate their abilities and performance, while women underestimate both. It's second nature for women to think they are "less than." In her book *Mindset*, Stanford psychology professor Carol Dweck talks about how women who struggle with failure fall prey to "fixed mindsets," or the belief that their abilities are static or permanent. An athlete would take a poor showing at a race or match as a personal criticism of her core self rather than a reflection of her performance that day. This only leads to low self-esteem.

Similarly, women tend to focus on our shortcomings rather than our potential; men don't. How do I avoid this? By recognizing that fear is normal, and you can't bypass it; the only way to deal with it is head-on. So focus on your best, don't compare yourself to others, and remember that fear is only a thought, *not* a reality.

What has helped me through the years is going back to the basics. It's okay to fail a lift or movement, because that's an opportunity to learn and grow and see what your capabilities are at the specific point. When you stop worrying about what other people think, you start to live your own life. That is when you become free to reach your full potential. Always come back to your why.

My fellow female CrossFitters, live fearlessly.

After those 2016 Games, as Shane and I drove out of Carson, California, we talked. And talked. We decided in our Hertz rental that we would never make the same mistake twice. We were no longer just happy to be there. From this point on, we needed to be dialed in. The question shifted from how to be great to how to be unstoppable.

At that moment, it crystallized for me that mental performance was just as important as physical performance. It was a shift that would change my trajectory. While this was a hard time for me, it was an important time to reflect. If it hadn't been for me coming in second, I don't know what the future would have looked like. Second place made me see that I wanted first place. As much as it still infuriates me that I went through all this disappointment, I realize that I needed to, because it has since fueled the fire that gave me the capability of winning. I was able to turn it around, and I now look back with no regrets. I know there were learning curves and they have made me into a better athlete today. I feel confident that it wasn't my physical ability that let me down in those first two years of competing—it was my mind. It hadn't quite caught up with my body.

Before we could make big changes, though, we had to rush off to the Rio Olympics, which were held in August, just a couple of days after the CrossFit Games. (Crazy, right?) In the end, I came in 14th for Australia, not a bad showing for a first-timer. Wearing the green and gold was a dream come true, regardless of the outcome, and I walked away from the Olympics with my head held high. I had a feeling of satisfaction that gave me a whole new outlook on life and how to approach things moving forward. More than ever, I believed I could achieve whatever I set my mind to, if I really wanted it. And winning the CrossFit Games was what I really wanted.

After we got back to Australia, Shane and I started working. We restructured our training program from head to toe—we changed everything from our coach-athlete communication (such as more positive reinforcement), workout program (less volume but more intensity), and schedules (no more overcommitting). It was a full-throttled strategy for obtaining what I missed out on that year—first place. We watched old videos, looked at my body language, observed my competitors, and critiqued my training habits, all to see where I could improve. No longer would I limit myself. I needed to give it absolutely everything.

Embrace Failure

Contrary to popular opinion, failure is not a bad thing. Failure allows you to keep pushing and keep evolving. Shane says on a daily basis: "Push as hard as you can. It's okay to make mistakes or fail. I guarantee you, it's at these moments you learn more about yourself, and when you learn, you grow." If you are only settling for the same back squat or the same row time, you're clearly doing nothing to progress. If you do the same, you stay the same. And that's not good enough when you want to be a champion. I often see athletes chase their old personal bests and when they get a moment to beat it, they settle for their old best or are satisfied with 10 pounds less. To me that means you're never going to get stronger physically and certainly not mentally. There is a place I like to call the "edge." It's a place where you push yourself enough to get to that edge where you may fail. Sometimes it's okay to go over the edge and fail, because you're only challenging yourself even more. But you have to understand where that line is and push yourself every time. I also look at fear of failure as a measuring stick to ensure that I am constantly pushing my abilities. Fear keeps you on your toes. It keeps you wanting more. As Mike Tyson once said about fear: "[It] is your best friend or your biggest enemy." So true.

There is a concept from James Clear's best-selling book *Atomic Habits* that speaks to the same idea: "Humans experience peak in motivation when working on tasks that are right on the edge of their current abilities—not too easy, not too difficult to pull off." I totally get that. This is the same edge I think about all the time. Much like the line between fear and confidence and success and failure, you need to walk a fine line to keep at the top of your game. Now go find your own edge.

Since I train with other athletes, I can recognize when they may have the same misunderstandings about fear as I had. It doesn't matter how experienced they are—I have seen this from the best of the best to younger athletes who are still trying to figure out their true capabilities. I can see that they're tightening up or thinking, *I don't want to mess this up* or *I don't think I can do this*. Just as I was petrified of doing the pegboard in that first competition, they, too, are scared to try something they are unfamiliar with. I let them know that I, too, had those thoughts, but I realized that I didn't need to fear failing anymore because failing is part of the process. Risks are exactly that—risky—but if you don't take any, then you won't get any better and you won't achieve your goals. Look at failure as a step closer to a win. Having made that mistake you will know not to do it again, giving you a leg up the next time.

Choose the Harder Option, Always

If there is ever an ounce of doubt, I always choose the harder option even if that means that I'm going to fail more in training. When I am lifting, sometimes I'll think, "Should I do 150? Or 155?" Well, 100 percent of the time I am going to go to 155. Because if I go heavier, it's going to make me better. The same goes for fear: Whenever I have an ounce of doubt, and I have a choice between an easier option and a harder one, I always choose the more challenging one. That's what was ingrained in me from the very beginning by my mum and dad. Because if it were easy, everyone would be doing it, right? And if you choose the easy option, you have to ask yourself: Do you really want it? I will always face the hard stuff. It's more daunting to go after the difficult choice than to go after the easier one.

TIA'S TIPS FOR STARVING THE BAD WOLF

1. Remind yourself that fear is good. When fear enters your thoughts, you will be at a crossroads: Play it safe or attack and chase progress. What will you choose? Look at fear as a great opportunity and lean into it. This attitude is something I had to learn to embrace—you are choosing to be uncomfortable, and that is not easy. I highly encourage you to keep challenging yourself because you never know what you're truly capable of until you put yourself out there.

2. Visualize yourself as a champion. We'll talk more about this in the next chapter, so remember this: This is an immensely powerful tool in helping you change your perspective. Try it—it will immediately change your mindset to a winning one and give you the focus needed to achieve your goals.

3. Prep, prep, and more prep. The more prepared you are, the fewer doubts you will have.

4. Have a mantra. Have a go-to phrase to help you stop negative thoughts. I often go to the popular Navy SEAL quote: "Fall to the level of your training." This line reiterates that you have done this a million times, and there's no reason for you to tighten up.

Take the Word *Procrastination* Out of Your Vocabulary

I believe procrastination is a killer of momentum. The longer you procrastinate on something, the harder it will be to build the momentum and the more likely you are going to struggle in your journey. Procrastination gets you nowhere. It only holds you back.

I was never much of a procrastinator. As you have read, my dad was a big believer in facing your fears, so I grew up being able to tackle any problem head-on. And, besides, I hated the stress when something was lingering over my head. But I do know people who struggle with it, and sometimes it is not all on them: Studies have shown that people who procrastinate tend to have high levels of anxiety or often feel overwhelmed and stressed out. If you are someone who suffers with this, is there something else that may be causing you to stall out?

Stay in the Moment

I grew up with parents who showed me how to live in the present. Maybe you didn't come from a family where this was ingrained in you, so saying to yourself, "Stay focused on the here and now" or "Just do it" may not be easy for you. That's okay. It's never too late to learn. Take my training partner, Brooke, who suffered a severe elbow injury during a heavy barbell snatch at the 2021 CrossFit Games.

She had surgery—what they call Tommy John surgery—and because of the long recovery time, she had to put her training on hold for 8-plus weeks. Returning to it was tricky—she needed to gradually work her way back into training, one step at a time. I could see that she was a bit overwhelmed by the process. She was looking down the long road of recovery and felt beat on day 1. I get it. I sometimes catch myself making the mistake of looking all the way up to the top of the mountain from the first step in front of me, too. When I am starting a new training cycle—which is 12-plus weeks of the season—I try to stay focused on the present moment, taking things as they come, because if I worry about weeks 10 and 11, even before I get through week 1, I am in trouble. So I felt for Brooke when she was struggling at the gym. She was trying a movement that she hadn't done since her surgery. Everything was daunting, and she didn't want to reinjure her elbow. She was doubting herself; you could see it in her face.

I told her, "Brooke, focus on the here and now, and be present. Just embrace what's going on right in front of you. Take your time. Just give me one rep. One single rep . . . okay, cool. We got through one rep, now let's just do another one. . . ." And, just like that, we simplified it and broke it down into individual movements. She didn't overthink the whole workout. She thought about that one particular rep that she needed to do. One. At. A. Time. She did six reps, and she said, "Wow, I pulled up really sore, but I did it." It was a "good" sore—her muscles were working and getting stronger. (Cut to the 2022

CrossFit Games—Brooke dominated and finished the competition in fifth place, exceeding everyone's expectations. I couldn't be prouder of her.)

When you're feeling overwhelmed by anything—whether it is coming back from an injury (or coming back from pregnancy!) or trying something new—try to break it down into short, manageable, tiny little goals. Then focus on each task of the moment; don't look back, don't look forward. Concentrate on what is in front of you, because if you make it too complicated, you will start to get overwhelmed, and any progress you did make will take a backslide.

Win Unapologetically

Consistency, preparation, and hard work are three principles that should keep fear at bay. And be proud of your work ethic. Years ago, I would never have been able to admit it. I was so "Australian" humble that I wouldn't have been able to say, "I'm the hardest worker," because I felt that I hadn't earned my stripes yet. I hadn't done my years, I thought. But over time, I've proven myself. Even though, deep down inside, I knew I was the hardest worker, I didn't want to be disrespectful to any of the veterans of the sport. I believe I've now earned the ability to say that I am the hardest worker in the room. It took me a really long time and a lot of push from the media to say so. I was so conscious of being considerate because everyone thinks they work hard, right? More importantly, this taught me a lesson—never be afraid to win unapologetically. You don't need to "earn it" by the years you tried—damn, if you are strong and fierce the first year in competition, go for it. Don't put limits on what you can do—go get that gold. I just wish I had listened to those who said that to me when I was first starting out.

The very first time I went to the CrossFit Games, a TV production company that was filming the Games had all the competitors create a video introducing themselves. I had to say into the camera: "I'm Tia-Clair Toomey and I'm the fittest on earth."

I thought to myself, *I'm not gonna say that. Why would I?* I haven't earned the right to say that. I did it, but it felt unnatural for me because I felt that the only person who deserved to say that was the person who actually won. You have to earn that. It wasn't because I didn't believe it, it was because I hadn't achieved it. Yet.

Over time I came to understand that Americans like to be vocal about winning. In Australia, it's more about staying humble and not necessarily expressing what you want to do, who you want to be, and the success you want to attain. Saying that kind of stuff aloud is considered arrogant. Aussies would go all Tall Poppy Syndrome and use sarcasm to cut someone down to size. For example, they would say back to a bold optimism, "Oh really, is that what you think you can do?" I now know that kind of talk is degrading to someone who is really just putting themselves out there.

I have definitely earned it now. And I think a piece of me has tried to adopt the "American" way after all the years I have been immersed in its culture. Why? Because I have come to appreciate their approach to winning. There is no need to be apologetic for your talent or drive. I suspect that Americans and other people might have viewed my reserve as insecurity or lack of confidence. But let me be very clear: That wasn't the case at all.

KEEPING OUT THE MENTAL CREEP

Thoughts often have a way of creeping in when you least want them to. Here are a few tried-and-true ways I have used to stay out of my own way when I am going for the win.

Don't think too far ahead. Stay present. Once you think ahead, you begin to overcomplicate the situation. One rep at a time.

Calm the inner critic. Think of the great Ted Lasso quote: "Be a goldfish. They have 10-second memory." If you fall off the balance beam, you move on. Always have that tape on **PLAY** not **REWIND**.

Just as you shouldn't look down or back while doing a pop-up on a surfboard or doing a routine on a balance beam, always look forward. And I mean this in both the physical sense and the mental sense.

Turn Fear into Fuel

Your emotions are so powerful. When I compete, I use my emotions as superpowers. I'll use anything that is going on outside or inside the arena to get me fired up—maybe it is an article that I didn't like or a slight by another competitor that annoyed me. And while I never really compare myself to my competition, there is an occasional reminder of a younger athlete hot on my heels. They are merely minor infractions and nothing personal, but I'll use all these provocations to my advantage. I'll build an internal dialogue that turns that anger or resentment into motivation, which helps me do a rep that much faster or hold on to the bar for that much longer. So bring it on—when it comes to competition, I'm out for blood.

Case in point: After the first day of the 2022 CrossFit Games, I was in eighth place. I had a tough time during the third event, making a rookie mistake that lost me time and ranking. I was angry. And I was upset that people were using that error to write my obituary. *Nope, that is not happening.* At the end of the day, when I spoke to Nikki Brazier, a CrossFit Games reporter, I let her know how I felt: "I'm looking for a fight. I can't wait."

The next day, I brought my A-game and took back the competition.

Those naysayers—those who thought they were witnessing the fall of a champion and spent that first day of competition questioning—*Is this it for her? Has she lost her dominance?*

Is her reign ending?—did me a favor. All that negative talk just fired me up. Some people like to tune out negative comments; I don't. I turn the negative into a positive, and use it as fuel for the next day's events. I won't apologize for that. So, it was the worst thing they could have done if they wanted to throw me off. I came back the next day into the arena roaring. Bottom line: You know what you need to do with all the energy you used to feed your fear? Use it to strike fear into your opponents.

I was not going to have my dominance questioned. I may have had a bad day, but I still had my eyes on the prize. I had trained myself to think that all these people next to me were my rivals, and I didn't want to give them an ounce of hope that they were going to come anywhere near me. I wanted to show them that, even though they may have worked hard, they were not even close to where I was capable of going. I have a lot of respect for all my competitors, but if they were going up against me, they would have to bring their best to the floor. Even then, I would never let them beat me.

We all have battles to fight, so why fight with yourself? No one else is going to believe in you. You need to believe in yourself, and those people who have it in for you—those who think you are going to fail—won't ever have your best interests at heart. And I can guarantee that because I triumphed despite those people trying to bring me down. So go ahead. I dare you to keep doubting me, because I'll prove you wrong every single time.

Embrace the Naysayers

This is my secret weapon. All that negativity, doubt, and underestimation from others is just great fodder for me. When I compete, I use all that emotion deep down inside me and turn it into fuel that keeps me going. All those years of sweat and dedication to the process come out in one single power move as I use that fuel and prove everyone wrong—those who have ever questioned my ability or said I wasn't good enough or tried to spin stories about me without even knowing me. It's important to remember, though, that while turning a negative into a positive can be a powerful force, you don't want to do something that is filled with resentment. I only use it to up my game, nothing more. (*Note*: You will read this book without coming across the word *sacrifice* anywhere except here. Because nothing I do is seen as a sacrifice. *Sacrifice* means giving up something, and we don't see CrossFit as giving up anything. Dedication and sacrifice are two very different things.) No resentment here.

The more successful you become, the more naysayers you'll have—believe me. So while you may have a great support team, you will need to arm yourself against those who want to bring you down. CrossFit is a great community. Don't get me wrong—I love the sport because of how democratic it is and how supportive everyone is. But every industry has its haters—I am only talking about 2 percent of CrossFitters, but they exist. And they tend to be the loudest in the room. Be strong-minded, and tell them to go sod off—in your head, of course. I am not one for letting people know how I feel. If I am confronted with negativity, I will be professional, but I need to put that bad juju somewhere. I definitely experienced a lot of people saying that I didn't have what it takes—I was from the bush, I wasn't incredibly connected or backed by a well-known sponsor, take your pick. I also wasn't a recognizable face when I first started, so nobody gave me the time of day. These slights gave me motivation to show them just how wrong they were. And while some may say that's the wrong motivation, I say it can be exactly the thing you need to win.

When I came in first in 2017, I proved that you can make fear work for you. I proved that you can turn all that negative talk into positive energy. I proved that you can win unapologetically. As the exhilaration of being on the podium wore off, a new feeling settled in. *I'm right where I need to be. I put in the hard work. I've done everything I need to do to be at the top of my game.*

CHAPTER 4

Unstoppable Mindset

Think Like a Champion

Coming from a small, rural town in Australia and entering the big pool of American CrossFit athletes was quite a culture shock. At first, I didn't feel that I was in the same league as they were. But I learned that it didn't matter. What *did* matter was looking at myself differently. I had to look at myself as a champion rather than a mere participant. I had to see myself as embodying the character, skills, and discipline to achieve greatness. This change in thinking was crucial to my success. How you see yourself is how others will see you.

That doesn't mean you are going to win all the time. You are always going to have days when you are hurt, fall short of your personal best, or lose to an opponent, but don't give in to the temptation to feel sorry for yourself—those moments will make you unstoppable. This mindset is multifold: Be selfish (in a selfless way), be humble, be relentless, be kind, and be a good sport.

Be Selfish

I admit it. I am eager to please. When I was growing up, I had a circle of friends at school, and we always ate lunch together. When we were done—before we went off to play—we'd have to take our lunch boxes to the back of the room. One girl knew how to work me, so she would say to me, "Because you're a fast runner, can you go and take my lunch box down to the back?" She thought she could flatter me into doing it. It worked the first time. "Oh, sure." I liked helping my friends out. But then it became an everyday thing, and I felt like I was running around at her beck and call. She started encouraging others to do the same—they knew they could take advantage of me. And they did. Although I never said anything to them, I did question it enough to eventually ask my mum one day after school, "Why does everyone make me do everything?" She suggested I stop hanging out with them if they made me feel that way, but at the time I felt like I had no other choice. As I matured, I realized that we all have a choice. People will take advantage of niceness if it is perceived as weakness, consciously or subconsciously. So while, as kids, my friends may not have consciously known they were doing that, you can either allow people to hurt your feelings and dictate your actions or not.

This default mode of mine was identified by Miles Wydall,

my weight-lifting coach early in my career, months before I even knew what was possible. One day—I don't remember what had prompted him to do so, but I can only assume I let someone go before me when it was my turn in a movement—he said, "You know, Tia, if you want to be as successful as these other athletes, you are going to have to become more selfish."

He must have seen my perplexed look as he continued to explain what he meant: "There is going to be a time when you have to choose whether you want to give other people your time and energy or you want to keep that for yourself and put that energy into developing your own abilities."

I thought about that comment for a while. I've always thought there's no reason to be disrespectful or selfish to those who have helped support me. Because if it wasn't for them, I probably wouldn't have been able to achieve what I have. So, I always felt I had to show my gratitude. I wanted them to understand how much I valued their efforts and company. But the more I thought about it, the more I understood what he meant. I was always putting other people's needs before my own. I realize now that I don't have to change who I am as a person to be an unstoppable force on the competition floor. Being selfish in order to attain my goals is not necessarily the same thing as being disrespectful. But when I compete, I put myself first—so I can finish first and stand on that top podium in any competition (after congratulating my fellow competitors).

It's a concept that is constantly evolving. In 2020, as Shane and I began an online fitness platform company called PRVN Fitness and as it grew rapidly, he started coaching a lot more athletes than just me. I saw it as an opportunity to help others achieve similar success—I love to share me experiences with others who have the same ambition and passion as I do, and I do so more as a mentor than as a coach (Shane has that part down pat). But I also know that this can interfere with my own training, and I have to be careful how much time I dedicate to others. For example, throughout the entire 2021 season, I helped fellow CrossFitter Brooke Wells develop as an athlete, and in 2022 I continued helping her and added another CrossFit athlete, Saxon Panchik, to the roster, among other athletes aspiring to make it through the season. I was so excited to help out fellow competitors, but, in doing so, I compromised my own focus. Don't get me wrong: I don't regret my decision, but I would be in the middle of a workout myself and I would start thinking about what the others were doing. I'd stop short so I could debrief them about how they could shave off a second on their workout or be more efficient on the barbell. I pride myself on being able to share my experience with others, but it took my attention away from my own performance. It wasn't until the 2022 CrossFit Games that I realized I wasn't as dialed in on my own performance as I would have liked to be. Lesson learned. While I wanted to be a force of support, I needed to make sure I was my number one priority. Being more selfish with my time is a necessary part of being a champion.

Be Humble

Okay, so here is the tricky part. To be on top of your game, you need to be selfish, but you also have to be humble. People misinterpret the humility part of competing—they think that being humble means you're a pushover or meek, the way I now see myself as a young girl being manipulated by my so-called friends. And it reverberated a bit in the first year I won the CrossFit Games. With my first win, after coming in second twice in a row, there was a mad dash by CrossFit media folks to get an interview with me. And here I was a rookie in dealing with the media, with absolutely no experience in front of cameras. I did my best, but because I was so green, I came off as timid. When I watched one of those interviews, I was mortified, to say the least, at how I came across. I had grown up with so much confidence as a young girl, especially in sports—otherwise, I wouldn't be where I am today. That didn't change how the producer wanted to portray me, and I am still haunted by those early clips because they don't show the truth. Yes, I was a rookie, but I was also a rarity. Athletes qualifying for the Games after only having done CrossFit for a few months were basically unheard of. I had literally done one small local competition, and then, next thing I knew, I found myself at Regionals and then at the CrossFit Games, completely unexpectedly. That took confidence. That took drive. So when I watched those clips, I barely recognized myself. My humility was mistaken for timidity.

At the time, I never wanted to brag or boast about what I do or who I am. I just wanted to go out there and test myself. But I realized that being too humble was holding me back. It limited my power. So I thought, *The heck with this. I'm not going to just wait for things to happen, I'm going to make them happen and not apologize for putting myself out there.* And that is when I started taking notes on my adopted country and became more American and self-possessed.

I'll just drop in this quote from the entrepreneur and author Andy Frisella, who while I was a guest on his REAL AF Podcast, defined *humility* perfectly: "It can be your best friend or it can bury you. You have to know when to flip that switch from 'I'm here to learn' to 'I'm here to execute.' Those are two completely different things. In order to do anything better in life, you need to be open to learn and be humble. When it's time to execute, you execute. . . . Just recognize that there's a lot of humility that went [into everything that led up] to that moment. A lot. Otherwise, [you] couldn't have gotten that good."

Be Relentless

I have heard several CrossFit athletes say that they don't compete just to participate; they compete to win. When I first heard this, I thought it was sad because they seemed to imply that they don't enjoy the experience. But now that I've gone from upstart to defending my place atop the podium, I have changed my mindset from "I'm so glad to be here" to "Attack, Attack, Attack!"

I still love every minute of it; I am just more aggressive now and I know what I truly want. And the day that I stop attacking is the day I turn into defense mode, and when that day comes, I may as well hang up my trainers (sneakers to you Americans). So, from day one to the last day of competition, I *will* attack every single moment on the floor. It's all part of being a champion.

Be Kind

There is a term in CrossFit for people who are kind to others: firebreather. It's someone who works hard and may finish fast, but sticks around to cheer everyone on. That is the beauty of the CrossFit community.

It's okay to be selfish while you're in the heat of competition or reaching for a goal. You don't have to be best friends with everyone, and, frankly, it's just hard to get to know a person during competition as everyone is so dialed in and you don't want to use your energy for anything other than executing your workouts perfectly. But now that I am a veteran, I try to make sure I am both encouraging of my competitors and still relentless. There is a time and place for support.

The way I see it, there are two Tias: the one at CrossFit Games trying to dominate, and the other Tia, who for the other 51 weeks of the year is "normal" Tia. During the Games, I have my game face on, physically giving my all on the floor and doing absolutely everything I can to maximize my performance for that week. I don't have time for small talk.

Back to the difference between US and Australian sports: I am generalizing a bit here, but the American attitude tends to be that hard work pays off, which is so true, but how we get there is different. I find that Americans tend to be much more individualistic and Australians are way more collaborative. It is just a different perception of success, but I have come to believe that, yes, you want to have a killer instinct, but *only* when you are on the clock, not off. Ever. But don't ever mistake my kindness for weakness.

While it's all about blood on the floor, it is all about heart *off* the floor. I have to admit that sometimes my passion can be mistaken for aggression. I have learned over the years that I need to be aware of how people may perceive me—they may mistake me as that intense competitor at all times. As a champion and now someone in a leadership role, I needed to step up and be more cognizant of how I came across. So, I started to take full responsibility in leading by example. Although I have trained vulnerability out of myself, because of the nature of competition, I have had to learn to bring a bit of that back so I can be more empathetic to others. It is a constant balancing act. Success—and the responsibility that comes with it—has all been a learning curve for me, but I have worked through how I can translate it into being unstoppable.

Be a Good Sport

Since getting into CrossFit, I have definitely come across people who feel threatened, jealous, and resentful. I don't want to be specific here, but it's fair to say that we can recognize when these people feel disappointed in their own performance and lash out, but that doesn't mean that we should stoop to that level. They may even take it out on you, but always show grace. Understand that it happens and that it is part of competition, and do your best to ignore it. If anything, if someone feels threatened by you, well, you must be good, right? So use that and show 'em that they *should* feel threatened by your ability. Speak through actions as opposed to speaking through words.

I saw all kinds of sportsmanship as I grew up. As I got better and faster at my running, I progressed from local to district to regional to state and national level. At every stage, there would always be someone new I'd be competing against and later stand next to on the podium.

Dad always reminded me, "Tia, when you go and compete and there are girls better than you, be happy for them, as you would want them to do the same for you. Always make sure you congratulate them." So I wished my competitors good luck and always congratulated the winner.

At my state championships in 2004, I had won first place, and as I walked over to the podium to get my medal, I smiled at the second-place winner. Rather than smile back, she just stared straight ahead as she stood on her spot. She didn't congratulate me; she didn't acknowledge me at all. I get it, so many emotions can run through your mind when you are disappointed in yourself, but it's not a great look when you can't be happy for other people's success. She may have felt that she let herself down, but I have always believed it's just as important to applaud other people's efforts. She wasn't the only one. There was another fellow runner at school who would always win, but she would never be gracious about it. It wasn't what she said, it was what she didn't say. She would barely even look at me. I was a threat, I get it, but I naively thought, *Wow here's another girl into running—perhaps we could run together, train together, pump each other up. Okay,* I thought, *so maybe she wasn't interested in being friends,* but I truly didn't understand why she just couldn't be happy for the athletes who beat her.

Once after one meet, as I walked to the car with my dad, he turned to me and said, "Tia, there's no point in you standing on top of the podium and being the champion if you're not a good sport. I don't care who you are, what you've done, where you are. Always make sure that you give the other athletes respect, because, at the end of the day, we are all human beings. Treat people as you would want others to treat you." (He'd often bring my sisters along, so he could point to them and say, "Think of how you want your younger sisters to be treated.") You always want to show good sportsmanship. Wish everyone good luck. Congratulate the winner on a win. Sportsmanship is important because it really shows who you are as a person. Traditionally, sports aren't meant to be a ruthless, cutthroat pastime. It's entertainment—where people shine and show off their talent and their drive. Sometimes people forget that.

As a rookie to the Games in 2015, I had no idea what to expect—it was the first time I was exposed to the world of CrossFit, especially outside of Australia. The facility and the sheer vastness of the stadium blew me away. It was like going to my first day at a new school: I was shy and reserved and didn't know any of my Australian counterparts. I walked into the arena feeling totally out of place. To me, I was a small-town weekend warrior from a small CrossFit affiliate, surrounded by people who were much more qualified to be there than I was. But one athlete went out of his way to make me feel welcome: Noah Ohlsen. He had already built a name for himself in the CrossFit world, so it was one face I was certainly familiar with. He came up and introduced himself and asked about Shane, which shocked me because I didn't think anyone knew who we were. I doubt he would remember this encounter, but it is one I'll never forget. He made me feel so much more comfortable in an uncomfortable environment, at a very important moment in my CrossFit journey. To make someone feel good about themselves and make them feel like they're a part of the experience goes a long, long way. Those moments when you stick around to cheer on a competitor or welcome a rookie add to your being a complete champion.

It is possible to be both insanely driven on the floor—with little time for niceties—and completely supportive off the floor and on the sidelines. Roger Federer is the perfect example of a good sport. In the 30-plus years he has been playing tennis, he has always delivered and provided a very high level of professionalism and class.

He's always shown a lot of respect to his coaching team, to the umpires, to the tennis organization, to his fans, and, last but not least, to his competitors. He has been so successful that no one would blame him for being a prima donna, but he just always showed up and did his job. And even when he was under pressure, he kept a level head. In his last tournament at the Laver Cup in September 2022, there was a picture taken of him sitting with his longtime rival Rafael Nadal (they played each other 40 times), holding hands, both crying. What an image. That is the epitome of good sportsmanship.

I had another great influence at the 2015 CrossFit Games, when Shane and I traveled to San Diego early to acclimate to the climate of the Californian summer a few weeks before the Games. We had been looking for a chef to help with my meals, and we found one—he happened to be the personal chef of multiyear CrossFit Games athlete and former Navy SEAL Josh Bridges. Next thing you know we were invited to Josh's house to train and have dinner with him and his chef. My initial reaction was that there was no way I was going to bother one of the most popular athletes in the sport. He was one of my favorites to watch in the Games, not because he was so dominant in the sport but because he had such good character. The way he competed showcased the passion he had for the sport, and it never failed to get the crowd fired up.

I didn't want to impose, but I also knew how much I could learn from a veteran like Josh. Shane convinced me it was a great opportunity and so we went, and what was initially one dinner turned into a years-long friendship. I am still taken aback by his generosity in inviting us into his home that first time—and many other times that followed. He also invited me to come and train there close to the Games and let me ask him myriad questions. I was so worried that I was annoying him, but couldn't help but be a sponge. I took in everything he said as gospel. The mere fact that I knew Josh going into that year's Games gave me an even bigger level of confidence. I still didn't know many people, but Josh checked in with me every so often between events, as did Noah, which felt like a big brother move. When I came in second, he screamed, "What just happened?!" I could tell he was so happy for me.

I answered, "Maybe the training that I did with you the week before the Games really helped me get to the next level."

"Okay, I'll happily take that credit!" he joked. More proof he embodied what a great sportsman should be.

A WORD TO YOUNG CROSSFITTERS

When I first started CrossFit, I was 20. Today, the athletes walking into the gym are as young as 12, 13—and some of them started even younger! I look at them and feel old, of course, but also hope that they know that they are entering an exciting period of their lives. They are just developing and getting to know who they are and what they want to become. If this is you, take it from me: I, too, battled with how to present myself when on the field. Being so young, you may not have full confidence or know what you want yet; you are just figuring out who you are. If you are like me, you may come off as shy at first. That is okay. But if you want to be taken more seriously, you will need to build up that outward persona so it looks like you know what you're doing—even if you have to fake it for a bit—I assure you it will come more easily in time.

For example, I used to fall into the trap of speaking sarcastically or in a self-deprecating manner. I would often put down my performance or my stature. Let's say someone wanted to take a photo of me. My first thought would often be, *Damn, there's people who are recognizing me . . . that's so cool.* But my outward reaction would be to play it down and say something like, "Are you sure you want a photo with me?" I know now this came across as insecure. I started to realize that I needed to change that if I wanted people to perceive me in a stronger, more confident light. So I worked on this every time I was in public. I treated this as creating a good habit. I made an effort to be more purposeful in my interactions with others, knowing that it reflected on how they perceived me. Now, when someone wants to take a picture with me, I say yes, smile, and thank them for being in my corner.

Today, when I look back at myself, I can see that I was too young to understand the importance of the mental aspect of CrossFit. I put in the energy that was required to always be physically ready, but time and time again life showed me that inner confidence needed to manifest itself into an outer confidence as well. Nowadays, I'm the first to go and say hello to people. I'm still not always comfortable doing this, but it's something I've realized is important and I've made myself work at it.

If this is you, too, I promise you it will get easier with the more experience you have; through experience comes confidence. You are what you put out in the universe, and if you exude self-assuredness, well, then, you're going to be taken more seriously. And this is where good habits can help project a stronger, more confident image.

CrossFit Is a Sport for Good Sports

As I started to write this chapter, right after the 2022 CrossFit Games, there was some talk in the CrossFit ether about whether or not the sport needed a villain. CrossFit is a very young sport, compared to soccer, baseball, or football, and it seems to have gotten a reputation for being "too nice." Some feel that a bit of swagger and bravado could make CrossFit more exciting and attract more fans. I get it—a tiny bit. Cross-Fit has been largely devoid of a Conor McGregor or a Mike Tyson who can help elevate a sport into the mainstream. We live in a post–reality TV–Kardashian world, where success is measured by the number of social media likes you garner and the more outrageous behavior is what trends. But is that where CrossFit wants to go? To let big egos into the arena merely because it is more entertaining and it may sell more tickets? What happened to the beauty of the sport? I understand the compelling story in the more entertainment-heavy UFC and

WWE, and even aggressive bad boys in more conventional sports like soccer's Wayne Rooney and basketball's Dennis Rodman, but CrossFit is built on community first and foremost.

The Business of CrossFit

Of course, CrossFit is a business, and business needs growth. Professional sports are about individual personalities competing; when those personalities get traction in the media, that coverage can translate into public interest, which, in turn, can generate advertising dollars. For new sports like CrossFit, awareness—and the money that can follow—can make or break the sport. When the sport had its first competition in 2007, there were 70 competitors. In 2022, there were 294,980 athletes signed up for the Open. In 2007, the prize money was $500. In 2022, the prize money was $310,000. I know I am a cog in a growing wheel: The CrossFit name and the sport's sponsors have helped me build my brand, while I've helped build theirs. Shane and I relocated from Australia to America in 2018 because CrossFit is centered in the United States, but in time I'm hoping that the sport becomes bigger globally.

Part of this growth falls on the athletes to be visible outside of the sport, aligning themselves with good sponsors. So we need to be savvy in the athletic world and also in the business world, in efforts to support not only the individual athlete but also the entire ecosystem within CrossFit. We all have a responsibility to be part of that rising tide to lift all boats. To me, CrossFit champions rise from the local gym to the global stage community because like-minded athletes (for the most part) all believe in the notion of "checking your ego at the door" so there isn't much room for jerks.

In fact, CrossFit believes so much in the concept of community and the importance of sportsmanship that these are written into the CrossFit rulebook. For this reason, CrossFit is said to be one of the most friendly sports out there. That is what drew me to the sport in the first place—the camaraderie, the feeling of community, the inclusiveness. There is much to write about sportsmanship, about being respectful and graceful—but to be a true champion, I do think there is a balance—not being so meek that people walk all over you, and not being so selfish that you don't consider other people's feelings. So, perhaps UFC needed Rhonda Rousey and McGregor to become global, but hopefully CrossFit doesn't have to go over the edge of niceness to do so. Why can't it be that someone who wins the title seven times is enough to make it a world-renowned sport? CrossFit was built by athletes all over the world who came together to celebrate health and fitness, but found something deeper. If it is to remain, at its core, the very community-building, supportive, and inclusive sport it has built its reputation on, villains aren't encouraged to apply.

BE A SPORT

1. **Practice self-control.** It can get emotional out there on the field, but always make a conscious effort to control your emotions and focus on the game. I have no tolerance for people who yell, slam dumbbells down, or leave the room in a huff—that only spreads the negative energy around to everyone else in the room and is just disrespectful. Be cognizant of those around you.
2. **Win graciously.** Showboating is not a good look, nor is putting down other athletes. Thank your competitors, the organizers, the volunteers, and, most of all, your team. No one is better than anyone else in this game of life.
3. **Follow the rules.** Cheating, taking shortcuts, or bypassing the rules should disqualify you from the game of life.
4. **Show respect.** Shake hands whether you won or lost. It reminds you that this is just a game and your competition sweated just as hard as you did. Part of good sportsmanship is dealing with disappointment. Okay, so maybe you didn't win. That doesn't mean you are allowed to have a temper tantrum on the field. Respect your competitors—after all, they beat you—they were better than you (that day). A true champion acknowledges that, gives props to the winner, and moves on to the next challenge with dignity.

There was once a time when no one thought anyone could break the two-hour mark of running a marathon. And then it happened. The same thing with running an under–four-minute mile. No one could do it until one person did it. And then there were people who followed, shattering those records. And so on. I am the first person to win the CrossFit Games six times consecutively, but someone will beat my record one day. There will always be people out there who keep pushing the limits. My own life is living proof of that. If you are determined to go out there and give it hell—all while never forgetting to be a good sport—that is what an unstoppable champion is.

CHAPTER 5

You Are Your Weakest Link

Build a Great Team Who Are All in It Together

Funny story: I didn't know Shane was technically my coach for the 2015 CrossFit Games until three years later. When I first started doing CrossFit, I didn't know a snatch from a jerk, and Shane had little CrossFit coaching experience, so there was a *big* learning curve for both of us. But once I got the hang of it, we made a slight change of plans and decided to qualify for the Games in the middle of the Open in 2015. We figured it was best to outsource a coach who worked with previous Games athletes in Australia. We found someone with experience and I was pumped that I'd be working with them, and Shane was relieved to have help getting me into fighting form.

At some point into training, however, Shane was disappointed by this coach—he didn't give us as much guidance as we had hoped—but Shane let me think otherwise. He wanted me to think I was using the more experienced coach's program to build confidence in myself. Meanwhile, Shane took on the lion's share of coaching and programming. For what he didn't know about CrossFit, he made up in spades in doing research. Shane would go on YouTube and Instagram to watch videos from top-notch CrossFit athletes and tailor them to my needs. (For instance, for rope climbs, we would watch Jason Khalipa, and I'd watch Rich Froning for barbell cycling.)

So, years later, imagine my surprise when I learned that Shane was the mastermind behind my programming and coaching. "Oh, my God, why didn't you tell me?!" I asked him.

"Well, you needed to believe wholeheartedly in the program."

"What happened? Why didn't you think that he had good programming? Why did you allow me to take him on?"

"He is a great person with the best of intentions, but he was training others at the same time and I think he was stretched too thin. I didn't want to worry you."

I should have known. I could even tell that halfway through the Games in 2015, I was not the priority for this coach. In fact, on the first day, when he was supposed to be helping me warm up, he was getting treatment from a bodyworker in the warm-up area.

I often wondered if Shane had the coach's band (meaning he could be in the warm-up room with me) during the Games, would it have changed my result? Shane was brilliant—he still is, of course—and he did it quietly. He didn't want me to know so I would continue to think I was being trained by one of the best coaches in Australia. It was the only way to get my confidence levels up on the world stage. Contrast that with the other coach, who seemed to be in it just for himself.

Finding people who are selfless and who genuinely want to see you succeed is a key component to your success—in anything. In my now many years in CrossFit competition, I have met so many people who can be incredibly supportive, but I have also found some snakes in the grass, especially the more successful I became. I managed to steer clear of them by surrounding myself with a ride-or-die team. That team has stepped up and understood what it takes to be at the top. They know that while there are many sunny days, there will be some rainy days, and those are not days to make things about themselves or feel sorry for themselves. They accept the challenge and ride the wave. It's tough, because some people want praise or recognition for everything they do, but sometimes you don't get that until the job is done. I know I am successful because of the team I have around me. To build anything in life, you need to have a team you can trust behind you and believe in them so you can believe enough in yourself. If you don't believe or trust that you have the best team, then you're never going to believe in the work that you're putting in, and that's going to transfer over to competition.

We are all in it together, as in the saying "iron sharpens iron." It would be impossible for one tool to become sharper without the other. On their own, both would become dull over time. It takes more than just one person to be successful—it takes a team of good people. When you have the right people in your corner, they're helping you and vice versa—iron sharpens iron.

When you have clear support, there will be no second-guessing and no doubt about what you need to do. You can just come out and compete, trusting that the group behind you has your back.

This team will tell you what you need to hear, but they will also always have your best interests at heart and will give you that confidence and reassurance to go out there and absolutely crush it. You will know that you have the right people around you when they challenge you and make you better, pushing you to evolve, and vice versa—you push them as well to be their best. Some days you just want to take a break, but those are the days you need them to tap you on the shoulder and remind you that you can't rest if you want to win. (You don't have to be an elite athlete to have support behind you, either—your support could be a group of running friends or a collaborative intramural team. An encouraging force behind you is great to have at any stage of fitness and in any part of your life, really.)

It isn't always easy. I have had people in the past who have supported me and understood how grueling training and competing can be, and I have had others misinterpret my intensity as a sign that I am unhappy or never satisfied. It's fascinating that the same people who celebrate the wins can sometimes take the easy option of quitting when it gets hard and ugly. The cold, hard truth is that training isn't just nine-to-five; it's 24/7.

It's a grueling lifestyle, and when you come into my camp, I may be tough, but I can guarantee that as a team we will be standing on top of the podium at the end of the season. It will require you to step outside your comfort zone and challenge yourself—every single day, every single hour, every single minute. There is no such thing as weekends; there are rest days, but even on those rest days you are doing what you need to do to recover or mentally prepare for another hard week of training.

Know Yourself

I was fortunate that at an early age I had people who encouraged me in everything I did. I was able to try out all types of sports, both individual and team sports. I swam, played tennis, ran, and played netball (a typical Australian/Commonwealth country game—a combination of basketball and handball). Since I wasn't pushed into any one type, I was able to eventually understand how I worked best (probably to the detriment of my early teammates). For instance, when I took up netball in the seventh grade, I quickly got frustrated. I felt that a few girls weren't putting in the effort I thought we needed, and I felt that I had to make up for that, running the whole court. I would come home and tell my mum how I felt I needed to make up for everyone else's lack of effort. "Tia, that is what being part of team is—learning to lean on other team members, passing the ball, trusting them to do their part. . . . It's not up to you to run the game." Call it impatience or having unreasonable expectations, but I didn't enjoy relying on other people to help me get where I wanted to go. I didn't have the patience for all that. Looking back on it now, I must have been a daunting teammate (even at the age of 12!) and probably needed to chill out and just be content with "having fun."

I may have been hotheaded, but I did get the message: I am better off relying on myself to perform. However, that doesn't mean I am completely on my own. I have a team of people who have helped me throughout my journey and have had a great influence on my success. If it weren't for them and their support, I wouldn't be where I am today. Over the years, I have noticed that my journey is similar to the journeys of professional tennis players. We all work toward individual success, and there may be many hours of solitary training, but we all do so with a close-knit, supportive team and coaches. So I figured I have gotten the best of both worlds.

WHAT, ME, IMPATIENT?

Patience is in short supply in the world of ultra-competitive people—myself included. I have learned (the hard way) to manage this emotion—in a world of instant gratification, patience is indeed a virtue. Here is how I try to maintain my patience—whether I'm feeling that I plateaued in my dead lifts or I'm just waiting in a long line at the coffee shop.

1. Jot down the different situations that make you feel impatient. Ask yourself why these situations make you this way. Awareness is always the first step.

2. Focus on what you can control and what you can't. You can't really work any harder. Or can you?
3. Try to distract yourself. You can't make the coffee line any shorter, so can you multitask? Write that quick email back confirming a meeting? Or start listening to your favorite podcast?

Obviously, there is a different level of emotional support needed for team and individual sports, and I have a great appreciation for people who play on teams, because you have to handle and adapt to so many things that are simply out of your control. You have to learn to lean on each other, trust each other, and balance out the responsibility of carrying the team. When I was younger, I already had a big competitive streak and preferred to keep things under my own control (as in my netball days). As I've grown up, I've appreciated more about what goes into being a part of a team. And what I love about Cross-Fit is that while I compete as an individual at CrossFit, the Games are very community-oriented, and there are a lot of people who go into creating the person you see on the field. The team works well off the field, so, when I am competing, I only have to focus on myself.

As much work and effort as my team gives, I give back. They deserve my all if they give their all. They are accountable to me, and I am accountable to them.

What to Look for in Your Ride-or-Die Team

Get a Great Copilot

My secret weapon is Shane. Not only is he an incredibly good coach, he's someone I can count on to give me encouragement when I doubt myself, as well as serving a bit of humble pie when I get overconfident. Shane doesn't do it for the accolades or the attention or the potential money. I know 1,000 percent that I've got the right person in my corner. Yes, we are married, but we keep that very separate from the coach-athlete relationship. (For the most part; it's hard not to talk shop at home!) The amount of pressure that you are under can obviously bring out a ton of emotions—and I am not one to shy away from letting them out. He's the one with the level head, he's the one who can help me to calm down, tell me to let it go. With Shane in my proverbial foxhole, I know that if I do absolutely everything that he tells me to do, I'll be standing on top of that podium at the end of the weekend. (It was Shane, after all, who, after I came second in 2015, said we needed to compete again. I was quite content with doing the one year, not yet realizing how I could turn this into a career. He was the one who said we could win the Games.)

If you can find your Shane, who knows where you'll go!

WHAT DOES THE IDEAL COPILOT LOOK LIKE?

Someone who is selfless and encouraging

Someone who keeps you accountable, no matter how hard that is

Someone who will be straightforward with you and not afraid to tell you what you are doing wrong

Someone who never wants to get complacent and is constantly pushing you to get better

Someone who doesn't ask for anything in return (except for 110 percent effort from you)

Someone who can let go of their ego

. . . And a Great Crew

Shane often likes to say, "If you hang around five millionaires, you will be the sixth. If you hang around five broke people, you will be the sixth." Well, that holds true in all areas, not just money. Surround yourself with people who have a similar outlook and are as ambitious as you are. Pick each for a particular strength, for every individual on the team should have a particular job, and you want the best in each. Don't surround yourself with yes men and women; no matter how successful you become, have people who are going to give it to you straight every time. There have been people who have come and gone throughout my journey, but I have come to know that I don't tolerate tagalongs. I often say to prospective teammates: "I'm here because I have a job to do and if you want to be a part of that journey, awesome. As long as you put in the work with us, let's take over the world!"

Take a good look around you. Are you hanging out with people who constantly push you to up your game? Or do they take the piss out of your accomplishments and goals? Do they make you feel bad for wanting more? Do they understand what it takes to achieve your goals? Are they bringing the environment down when you're trying to lift it up?

DOES YOUR TEAM PASS THE SMELL TEST?

1. Do they give off positive vibes? Steer clear of negative people. In order to be positive, you need positivity around you.
2. Do they match your ambition? People who have the same work ethic as you do will help you get where you want to go.
3. Do they push you to do things beyond your comfort zone in a healthy way? You want people to press you to be better, stronger, faster, but not if it means compromising your mental and physical health.
4. Do they keep you humble while encouraging you to be your best?
5. Do you feel light around them? You don't need people who are always looking for recognition or just weighing you down.

Good Communication

Communication has always been a priority between me and Shane, and now it's a crucial element within our whole team. The ability to effectively provide feedback *and* listen is such a big asset, as is the ability to read another person's body language and the way they conduct themselves. It's a multifaceted interaction, based on respect, and it helps provide motivation and create a bond among the team members—a great formula for success. As a team, we depend on each other so much that I compare it to a chair—if one leg falls off, the entire chair goes down, effectively rendered useless.

Shane is great with positive reinforcement; he knows (with me, at least) that he gets more bees with honey than with vinegar. So he'll couch a correction within this kind of compliment: "Hey, you're doing a phenomenal job with your feet placement. I love seeing that. Give me more of that." I respond to that kind of constructive feedback much more positively than if he just criticized something he thought needed to be corrected. It encourages me to push harder rather than focusing on something I'm doing wrong. He coaches everyone differently, though, depending on how they respond to direction. He is attuned to different personalities and what works to get the best out of his athletes.

Shane has gotten to be an expert at getting the best out of people by his positive attitude, and that is even reflected in his body language. He oozes confidence—and that becomes contagious. And he continues to learn, constantly open to new things. He often consults with other coaches and others in the coaching environment, and, to this day, he is always trying to adapt and evolve. He even looks beyond CrossFit. Strength and conditioning programs have been around for many, many years. CrossFit hasn't, so there are a lot of plans and processes to strengthen and condition athletes already out there. It's just about finding them and utilizing them in the best way. That's why Shane has studied a wide range of sports training programs, such as those used in the NBA, the NFL, and triathlete training. Because of Shane's outreach, we have been able to meet and learn from some of the top trainers and athletes in their respective sports and incorporated some of their regimens into our own programming, mashing it all together to give us the best opportunity to succeed. For example, swimmers can hold their breath for minutes, so Shane has studied how to gain that incredible lung capacity. Gymnasts have gravity-defying balance, so we study that, too. Pulling all these strengths from different sports is so helpful in getting yourself ready for anything that a CrossFit program throws your way. Even the smallest trick can help cut seconds off the clock. Triathletes, for instance, use rubber bands to pre-clip their shoes so when they transition onto the bike, they can easily and quickly get on and start riding.

Who You *Don't* Want on Your Team

The Underachievers

Those who aren't on your level will not be able to help you raise yours. If people don't match my intensity, they are off the team. It's that simple. I get crazy obsessed with things that I'm after, and I know I can't get there alone. I need to depend on my team, but they have to be on the same wavelength, and I find it disappointing when people don't match me on and off the floor. I was reminded of this the hard way in the spring of 2021, when I received an email from the pilot of an Australian bobsled team. (I know, bobsledding in Australia? But we do our best to represent Down Under.) Did I want to join her in hopes of racing at the '22 Winter Olympics in Beijing? I thought, *Wow, what an incredible opportunity. And this will be a great test.* I had already been at the Summer Olympics for weight lifting, and who wouldn't want to have another shot? So why not aim for the Winter Olympics? With my running background, I thought I could bring a lot to the role of brakeman (the power behind the sled who sets the speed for the run). I just needed to make sure that I learned all the fundamentals. It was a short turnaround to be a part of an Olympic team in less than a year, so we needed to hit the ground running (no pun intended).

Once I am committed to something, I'm committed 1,000 percent. I am not one to come in and do something half-heartedly. With this endeavor, I came in making sure that they were going to get my absolute best—I even gained 20 pounds so we would be heavier, and in theory, the sled would race faster down the track. Training took me and Shane to Korea, Austria, Switzerland, United States, Germany, Latvia, Poland, Belgium, and Italy as we juggled bobsledding with CrossFit.

It was exhilarating going down an ice tube at 80-plus miles an hour. It was crucial for us to get a fast start, so I would explode off the block and sprint for about 15 to 30 meters, jump in, put my head down between my legs and just wait until I felt the end, crossed the finish line, and pulled the brakes, trusting my pilot to get us down safely and efficiently. I couldn't see anything outside of the track zipping by through the brake gap, and I literally had no control over what happened; I just put all my faith in my pilot in getting us down. Since it was up to me to pull the brakes, I actually had to memorize the track by feel.

Even though we had accomplished what we set out to achieve—to qualify for a spot to the 2022 Winter Olympics—it was extremely devastating to have our seats ripped out from under us. It's complicated, but the Australian selection committee decided to send only one team to represent the country.

It didn't help that we felt we had joined a team that wasn't as like-minded as we were about competing—and winning. There will always be times when team members don't see eye to eye, and on something as big as ambition, sometimes things have a way of working out for the best. There was a silver lining to this experience: Had we gone to Beijing and competed in the Olympics, I may not have been able to recover in time to successfully defend my title at the CrossFit games later that summer.

But I kick myself on a daily basis for not reading the situation better, and I wish I hadn't been so eager to make the impossible possible. However, I can walk away knowing that if it were not for Shane and me participating in the bobsled season, Australia may not have even been in a position to send an Australian bobsled team to the Beijing Olympics in the first place. So, we took comfort in that. And it was still a tight window to get back into CrossFit shape (literal shape as I had to lose weight), so there wasn't much time to be disappointed. Hard lesson learned.

The Takers

In any part of your life, you are always going to have people who don't have your best interest at heart. I'm talking about those who take take take from you and don't give anything in return. From coaches to colleagues, so-called friends, even family members, there are people who just think of themselves: They glom onto you for the wrong reasons—money, recognition, proximity to success. Then there are the snakes—those who really do want to see you fail or bring you down for whatever reason. You need to realize that they comprise only a small portion of people out there. Just be aware that you don't need to be suspicious of everyone; simply learn to sniff out people's intentions.

I've had to learn the hard way that some people weren't the right fit to be part of the team, so I've had to let them go. It's sometimes tricky to have these conversations, but it is for the best. You can't allow them to suck the energy from you and the room. I've had to make those hard decisions, but they're made knowing I was making the right decision for me and the rest of the team. The more experience I have, the easier it has been to recognize bad behavior and to move on from those relationships.

Remember, Ignore the Naysayers

One night in 2014, after I won my very first local competition, Shane and I were walking out of our gym in Australia when I heard someone calling after me. It was a coach of another competitor—I thought he was going to congratulate me on my win.

"Good work, Tia. Who would have thought you'd do that well?" he yelled out to us.

Wow, I thought. *That was condescending. What did I do to him to elicit such a reaction?*

"You have to remember that you haven't actually competed against the best in Australia yet, so don't get ahead of yourself," he added, as if his first comment weren't enough of a dig. My face got red hot, and I was about to say something that I probably should not repeat here, when Shane patted me on the arm, letting me know it wasn't worth it.

When we got out of earshot of the coach, Shane turned to me and said, "I am glad you didn't give him the satisfaction that he got to you, T. He is just probably upset that his own athletes didn't perform as well as you did."

I listened to Shane and walked away without saying a word.

Naysayers—I have no time for them. In 2015, I was at a breakfast table at that year's CrossFit Invitational with several female athletes when one remarked, "Well, you know, all these rookies, they just have rookie luck; they have no expectations. They can just go on the floor and compete and have fun. Whereas for us veterans, we've been doing this for years, and they have no idea what our bodies have gone through and what we're dealing with."

I was the only rookie sitting at that table.

Obviously, she was taking aim right at me. I chose to ignore it, but mentally noted that I would never become jaded and discouraging. There is no room for such negativity anywhere on or off the field, and it does nothing but cast a gray cloud over everything. No thanks.

HOW TO GET THE BEST OUT OF YOUR TEAM

Set expectations. If you raise the bar, your team will follow you and raise their bar, too. Matching work ethic and priorities will keep everyone on their game.

Take ownership. It's still on me how I perform, ultimately—my performance is not anybody's responsibility but mine, and I have to keep up the intensity level. If I make a mistake, that's on me—no one else. This is true outside of sports as well. It's important to take ownership of everything you do in life, even in the workplace. At PRVN, if something doesn't go according to plan or someone has made a mistake, it usually falls on me because perhaps I didn't explain the task at hand well enough. I step up and take ownership rather than blaming the employee.

Trust those around you. I surround myself with a team I trust with my life. If you don't trust that you have the best around you, then you're never going to believe in the work that you're putting in, and that's going to transfer over to competition. Olympic swimmer Michael Phelps has said when asked about this trust in his coach, Bob Bowman: "People ask me how I do my stroke: I really do not know. Bob tells me what I have to do and I do it."

Leave your ego at the door. We talk about being selfish in another chapter, but when it comes to your team, take that ego out of the equation. You need to really rely on your team to help you achieve your goal—you will lose them if you make it all about you.

A positive environment will foster positive reinforcement. You may have to give your team members feedback they don't want to hear sometimes, but it's what they need. And vice versa. People who have your best interest at heart will ultimately give you the confidence and reassurance to go out there and absolutely crush it.

Be on Someone Else's Team

Ever since Shane and I started PRVN, we've gotten all sorts of athletes who come into the gym wanting to train with us, and we recognize that we are becoming part of someone else's team now. While we like to team up with people who share our values and know what they stand for, it has been an honor to think that we can now return the favor and be a support for others on their own CrossFit journey.

In the past, I had been particular about what I share and who I share my training principles with, but in 2022 I felt ready to open up. Just before the season started, I said the following to Brooke as well as other athletes who had joined us, including Will Moorad and James Newbury.

"If we are really going to do this, we're going to do it together. After this conversation, I want you guys to walk away, and I want you guys to have a deep think about whether or not this is something you want to do, but I can guarantee you that if you commit to this team, we're all in it together for the rest of the season, and nothing is going to break us down. Because the more we train together, and the more we push ourselves, the stronger and fitter we're going to be."

A few years earlier, I would not have considered opening up my training to a direct competitor, purely because I was so driven in what I wanted to achieve personally. I was reticent to share Shane's attention with anyone other than my training partner and Shane's male athlete, Mat Fraser (Men's five-time

Fittest Man on Earth). But over time, as I matured as an athlete, I began to realize the importance of challenging yourself to be better, and having a like-minded athlete in my camp would do just that. With Brooke training alongside me, that would be a constant reminder that I was not the only one chasing that top spot. The better she becomes, the better I become as an athlete and, in turn, we would be pushing each other in ways we both never thought possible. By being more open-minded to evolving and expanding your team, you can create opportunities that are more accessible than before.

My decision to do this comes back to reevaluating my why: I see this process of mentoring the next generation of competitors as a way to evolve into a mentor while continuing to develop as an athlete. And Brooke and I have figured out how to build each other up to achieve all of our individual goals, as a team.

I am not sure what the future holds for me, but I do know I'm going to continue to be relentless in *everything* I do. Having the right team around me who are equally willing to put in the work means we are going to crush that future, whatever it holds. And I am not going to apologize for holding my team to high expectations—they will thank me when the work is done.

RULES OF THE GYM

The New Zealand Rugby Team, commonly known as the All Blacks, is easily one of the most popular and most successful rugby teams in the world, winning the Rugby World Cup in 1987, 2011, and 2015. They have a list of principles they live by, and Shane and I adapted them for our own gym. They contain core values that each person who walks through our doors should embody. For me, I love when people appreciate us and what we offer as a fitness organization. If people come to work out with us and show consideration and appreciation, then, in return, they are going to receive more from us.

THE SEVEN RULES

1. Sweep the gym.

Never be too big to do the small things that need to be done.

Before leaving the gym at the end of the day, no matter how good you are or what your role is, you stop and tidy up. It is an example of personal humility, a core value we have to be a part of this training group. We believe that it is impossible to achieve success without having your feet planted firmly on the ground.

2. Never settle.

When you're on top of your game, change your game.

Even at the pinnacle of success, look to do even better.

3. Train with purpose.

Understand your why & if you don't have one, find it & if you need help ask for it.

In order to evolve and be successful, you need to ask questions. There is never a bad question—questions allow you to better understand and be more prepared.

4. Take ownership.

Leaders create leaders.

We believe the development of leaders and the nurturing of character off the competition floor help to deliver results on it. Shared responsibility means shared ownership, high accountability, and trust.

5. Embrace expectations.

Aim for the highest cloud.

Go forward! Reframe your challenges into proactive goals. You have to be proactive at all times. Taking risks and responsibilities is one of the many skills you learn from the sport.

6. Enjoy the journey.

Keep it real.

Throughout the process, stay humble and remember where you came from, but also don't forget to look at the big picture. This journey is not life or death; enjoy the process and don't get lost in it. Stay true to who you are and what you want to be.

7. Train to win.

Practice under pressure.

The foundation for success on a competition floor is built in training. You win events in training. The ugly truth is that, in most cases, you get the results of your daily/weekly training efforts and commitments in the competition. Make practice your test, make it intense. Training with intensity accelerates personal growth.

CHAPTER 6

Perfection Is Unattainable

Stop Comparing Yourself to Others and Embrace Your Differences

As much as I support being your true self, I recognize that it can be tough in the trenches of real life. This is especially true when there are bullies around who revel in pointing out anything that doesn't hew to standard ideas (and, thankfully, what is considered "standard" seems to be changing). My first real encounter with bullying happened when I was 12 and had been running competitively. My body naturally became very lithe and streamlined. I was also at that awkward age when the hormones kicked in, and boys tease girls about anything and everything, but this wasn't regular teasing. I started getting comments that I looked like a boy. It made me angry, but I never said anything. I would instead wait until my mum picked me up at the end of the school day. I would get in the car and finally let the tears fall. "Mum, you know, Robbie called me a boy again. . . ." Now this kid was super short and had buck teeth at the time, but I would never ever say anything to hurt his feelings.

Mum would inevitably say, "Tia, don't listen to him. And remember when boys pay attention to you, it's because they like you." But I never quite got this because it never felt like a compliment.

I continued to keep quiet—until I couldn't any longer.

One day I was walking to class and heard another boy in my class yell out, "Hey, Tia, you use the boys' locker room or the girls'?"

I don't care what bathroom you choose to use or how you identify, but I reacted to his intent—and his intent was to hurt me. Something inside snapped and I went over to him and yelled, "Leave me alone!" and hit him pretty hard in his arm. I think he was too stunned to do anything but cry. All the teachers knew that he had been picking on me, so it was a long time coming. They let it slide outside of a stern phone call to my parents and detention the next day. That boy never bothered me again. (Now, I am not condoning any type of violence here, but standing up for yourself is important—not just for yourself but for other people they may bully.)

Being Vulnerable

I typically don't allow myself to be so vulnerable as to show my emotions, but that day I had had enough. And it's okay to be vulnerable. We women—historically speaking—have a lot of impossible beauty standards to live up to, while at the same time we're underestimated in our physical abilities. It sucks that we still need to think about it and talk about it in the 21st century, but here we are. Systemic discrimination is still here— women athletes for the most part get paid less, get less sponsorship money, and women's sports, on average, get less TV time and media coverage. It is easy to see how this perception of women being "less" trickles down to women athletes' feeling of "less than" in their respective sports.

And in the world of competition, while we may feel "less" in several ways, one way we are "more" than men is in how our bodies are scrutinized. Whether it's gymnastics, ice skating, tennis, or any other sport women engage in, women's bodies are endlessly dissected. And if anyone tells you different, they are lying. Although we are officially being judged by our power, strength, and skill, we are often judged by our looks, too. We should only be judged by what our body *can do,* not what it *looks like.* It is not something we should have to consider, but we do. Too tall, too short, too fat, too skinny, too muscular (and if you are too muscular, well, you must be on steroids!) . . . women can never seem to catch a break.

How does this affect your chances? If you don't feel good about yourself, you are going to doubt yourself, and that doubt and second-guessing will show up on the competition floor. It may affect your overall motivation and passion for the sport. It's hard enough to get out of bed when it's 20 degrees out and still dark; if you are not in a good place emotionally, it will be even harder to get out from under your covers.

So I am going to be really, really vulnerable here, and it's not easy to do because I've trained that out of myself for so long. I have steeled myself against such societal and professional stressors, and my experiences are pretty mild compared to some. I haven't experienced much pressure, discrimination, or outright harassment myself, and I have the CrossFit community to thank for that. I appreciate CrossFit's egalitarian philosophy—women get equal time, coverage, and prize money as the boys. That is very empowering.

Still, I want to address the issues that woman still face in professional athletics across the sports spectrum.

When I was growing up, I had my own body insecurities, especially as I went from running competitively to CrossFit. I grew up pretty confident, but when it came to my body changing, this was a whole new ball game. After years of having a "runner's body," I started to see changes. My twig-like arms, my traps, and shoulders all bulked up. I felt like that cartoon of the Incredible Hulk, where his muscles pop out of his T-shirt. I first hated what I saw, and I was sure other people saw it, too; I felt them staring at me in shops and thought they saw me as too muscular, too bulky, which brought back hurtful memories of grade school and Robbie. I started to feel self-conscious. Rather than feeling pretty, I felt manly looking. How could Shane find me attractive?

Now I'm a lot more confident in my body, and I have accepted it for what it is. I started appreciating the work behind my muscle definition. I also changed up my wardrobe so that it flatters my new shape. Rather than wearing a thin-strap dress, I would wear a thicker-strapped one that better suited my fuller shoulders. But more important than changing what I wore on the outside was how I was changing my attitude inside. To achieve my goals, I needed to stop bringing myself down mentally for the way I looked or worrying about what others thought, and focus on the way I was performing. And you know what? Those people I *thought* were staring at me thinking that I was too big, too manly—I now realized that they weren't thinking that at all. Their stares were actually saying, *Damn, you must be strrroongg.* (And they were right.)

All that said, I see the pressures females are forced to endure in other sports that typically showcase "graceful" skills and moves—like tennis and gymnastics. Just one example of many: GOAT Serena Williams had been widely derided for her muscles and power on the court early in her career, but she rose above the noise to become the most celebrated female tennis star in history. Gymnastics and ice skating also come to mind as sports that idealize the female form. Such high standards placed on young women inevitably foster body insecurities. One athlete who has been vocal about this is gold medalist Simone Biles. She has often talked about being self-conscious about building muscle, so much so that she started wearing a lot of jackets to cover herself up, and she even bowed out of the 2021 Olympics because of mental health issues, either directly or indirectly related to the pressure to perform but also to look a certain way. She is just one of many. And I'll bet there is a long line of female athletes we will never know because they were so affected by the pressure directed their way before they got too far in their careers. They couldn't subject themselves to such unhealthy standards any longer. Approximately 68 percent of female athletes said they felt pressured to be pretty in a study conducted by ESPN. Also, 30 percent felt that they looked too muscular. That's a lot of women going around hung up on how they look when they should really be celebrating what they have accomplished.

Compete, Don't Compare

While I was never a girly-girl, I do care what I look like, but not to the extent of *needing* to put on makeup. Maybe it was my upbringing—I was just a girl who wanted to run and play sports; my parents loved my wild side. Mum always told me that I didn't need to wear makeup; I had natural beauty. My priority is not to look great at the gym; I'm going to sweat, so who needs makeup running down your face when you're trying to work out? My priority is to train harder, so if I spend half an hour on my hair, that's half an hour less I'm spending in the gym. Hair is less important than reps, in my eyes. I prefer to sleep an extra half an hour rather than get up to primp myself. I look at these other girls who are well manicured, not a hair out of place, face full of makeup—they look gorgeous. Unfortunately, though, all that attention to their image will take away from their game. Maybe one of the reasons they're not on top of the podium is that all that time they spend fussing over their appearance is time lost front squatting.

I think a lot of women who get caught up in their image do so because they feel the need to compare themselves to other women. That just puts undue pressure on them to be perfect. While focusing on the things that are "imperfect," you are putting energy on the negative, not the positive. And you'll always be running at a deficit. What do I do? I try not to compare . . . but if I find myself doing so, I try to turn those differences into positives. For example, if I see an athlete who is bigger than me, she's going to be able to manage the heavier weights more efficiently. I think, *How do I compensate for this and look forward to the challenge instead of feeling defeated?* I answer by training specifically for those differences every day. It's in facing those challenges that you can overcome them and be stronger for them. And, believe me, when you beat that heavier athlete who can naturally lift more than you, you will feel so much more satisfaction.

All this is to say that I try hard to not compare myself to others. Some days I am more successful at doing so. Looking up to other women, getting inspiration from them, being a role model to others—that is a different story. That is a positive action rather than negative and getting down on yourself. Each of us comes from a different background and carries with us different experiences—my upbringing and my experience are very different from yours, and we should celebrate those differences in others rather than feeling "less than."

Social Media and Body Image

Instagram, Facebook, TikTok, and other social media platforms don't make it easy. These platforms help people one-up each other and create a life that probably doesn't match reality. Their posts are misguided attempts to get followers and likes, but at what cost? One athlete I follow posted an image of herself provocatively dressed, and I thought, *Well, I'm sure we all can look good in lingerie, but I am not willing to post it and make it public.* She will get what she wants—a lot more attention, but I'm not sure it's the right kind of attention. And those posts will inevitably bring some women down, because they may not feel as comfortable with their own bodies, and with any kind of criticism, their self-esteem will get hit hard. I love to see women proud and embracing their bodies, but I wish they knew that they didn't have to expose themselves on social media just to get attention; people will love them for who they are, not how they look. I see women (whom I personally know) posting spicy photos and videos on their social media platforms, but they are nothing like that in person. I guess they feel obligated to do it to generate likes. I know they are strong, encouraging, kind females who have so much more to offer, yet they feel they need to hide their real selves to project a more hyper-sexualized persona. Female athletes are much more than what they look like. It is so empowering to see a woman showcasing her strength in back squats rather than her backside. I know some people love posting racy photos—and more power to them— but I prefer to know that my followers come to my page for inspiration, motivation, and a deeper connection with me.

Don't get me wrong: For the most part, I am a fan of social media. I love connecting with fans of CrossFit as well as competitors, athletes, supporters, and friends. And it is also an incredibly powerful platform on which to build my brand and cross-promote sponsorships—there is no denying that. For better or for worse, it is part of our everyday lives. You have to take the good with the bad, including a big downside—the online trolls who creep in and comment (aka keyboard warriors). I guess the anonymity of it all makes them feel free to express whatever they want from behind their screens, but some like to critique my career, my last competition, even my last event. Sometimes it's not even about my professional capabilities, but rather what I am wearing or how my hair is styled (or not styled, ha!). Everyone is a critic. It is hard to read sometimes, but I try to stick to those people who give me encouragement instead of those who try to tear me down. But the more successful I became, the more people seemed to want to knock me off my pedestal. One crazy accusation claimed that I had taken steroids. To some people, it isn't natural for me to be as strong as I am, so that must be the reason. The first time I heard this, I was so upset—how dare someone accuse me of cheating? After years of daily beatdowns, I got used to it, and it also helped that Shane had a great attitude about it: He would tell me to take it as a compliment. If they think I got this body by chemical means, then, heck, they must think I am super human.

A Note about Sexual Discrimination and Harassment

When I was a little girl, all I really wanted to do was gymnastics. When I was five, my mum enrolled me in a beginner class, and I was over the moon. In the very first class, the coach—a man—instructed me to get on the balance beam for a demonstration. He insisted on holding my hand as we walked over to it in front of the 10 or so other kids. I didn't know why, but it struck me as weird—and wrong. *My mum and dad can hold my hand, but it feels weird that a stranger is doing it*, I thought. My mum didn't stay to watch this first session, so I asked her to come to the second one to watch. And it happened again. I realize that coaches sometimes have to touch the athlete to show proper form, like help them flip or turn correctly, but he insisted on holding my hand as we walked to every station, and he would always use me for the demo. I felt a sense of unease every time he was near me. I couldn't put my finger on it, but it just never felt right. I was so young, and I kept thinking, *What are you doing?* I didn't fully understand what was going on. I did have the wherewithal, after the third time, to tell my mum that I didn't want to go back. My dreams of being an Olympic gymnast lasted a mere three sessions, which was super disappointing because I really enjoyed the sport and thought I would have been pretty good at it with the right training. I did ask my mum if we could find another gym, but she told me that I would have to choose my gymnastics over my other sports if I were to really give it a go. Now that I think about it, I think Mum just said that because she was worried that I might be put in a similar situation. I was soon distracted by my other sports so I didn't dwell on this decision for too long.

I was lucky that, as a woman, I hadn't experienced much more than that—maybe that's because I am always surrounded by family and later, Shane, who always looked out for me. Maybe because I was competing in the young, forward-thinking sport of CrossFit rather than a more traditional sport. I do know there are others who are not so lucky. Fortunately, things are changing. Recently, there has been a reckoning throughout the sports world and beyond, most publicly from the Larry Nassar scandal in which much of the 2016 US women's gymnastics team courageously came forward with their stories of sexual harassment. It is not easy to undo years of a simmering problem, but while it continues, the more awareness we have can help us better recognize when it happens and help us better stand our ground if it happens to us or to others who can't speak for themselves.

Body for Two

Shane and I found out we were pregnant shortly after the 2022 CrossFit Games. Before becoming pregnant, I never put much thought into how my body would change and, more importantly, how *it will never be the same.* But, wow, now I know. I had worked so damn hard to build up this machine, so when my hips widened, my middle expanded, and my feet swelled, I thought, *Oh, my God, I didn't have a chance to say goodbye!* While I grieved for my old body, it certainly made me respect the miraculous metamorphosis it goes through to grow a beautifully healthy baby and help prepare me for giving birth. So I embraced the newfound curves around my hips, the cellulite that appeared on my thighs, the stretch marks that materialized on my stomach. Because, at the end of the day, the psychological impact of all those physical changes diminishes once you hold that bundle of joy.

It's funny, though. As I went through my pregnancy, I couldn't help but see how the feelings I experienced becoming a mum echoed the emotions I went through as I became a competitor.

Feelings of fear. Even though Shane and I had talked about starting a family, the timing of my pregnancy had come as a surprise. I was suddenly walking into something unfamiliar, just as I first started out in CrossFit. I was in uncharted territory. I didn't want to do anything that would jeopardize the baby growing inside me, just as I was afraid to make a mistake or perform poorly in a competition. Luckily, the 2022 Games were already over when we found out, so I could hit the PAUSE button on training. I kept up with exercising—and did not specifically train. I was just maintaining my strength enough to keep me fit so reentry into training wouldn't be too bumpy. I also had worried about the baby's health, even though pregnancy was completely normal. I felt relieved that I was not alone in this: When women get pregnant, a flood of hormones goes into overdrive to help us bond with our babies, as well as a sense of overprotection and worry. I was becoming a momma bear and loving it.

I read all the pregnancy books out there and had solicited many opinions about everything from prenatal vitamins to rest, but I tried to steer clear of those people who think they know best. (Someone once told me I would hurt my baby if I exercised.) Still, we received so many opinions from friends, family, and even strangers on social media that it was all overwhelming and it added to the fear factor. *Was I doing everything right during this pregnancy? Eating enough foods? Getting enough sleep? Was I stressing out too much, and could that affect the baby?* My mind was spinning, and it was beginning to feel a bit too much, so I had to make a conscious decision to roll back taking in so much advice. I needed to stick to the basics and just let my body be my guide. I needed to check in with myself—and only myself (and, well, maybe Shane and my doctor) to ensure that I was not pushing too hard while bench-pressing. Everyone is different, so what might work for one person might not be the solution for another. Trust in *your* natural instincts.

My passion lives on. I always thought the day I became pregnant would be the day I would turn a page and just focus on being a mum. As it turns out, that hasn't been the case. To my surprise, my fire to compete burns deeper than ever before. I didn't know this to be true until one day at the gym I found myself watching a male athlete whom I trained with on a regular basis. I looked at him while he was doing ring muscle-ups, and for the very first time in my life, I felt jealous. Wow, I thought, as a guy, he can continue on uninterrupted in this career. He has two children of his own, but he never had to give up a season, whereas I had to sit out because I physically could not compete. While I understood the bigger picture of having a healthy pregnancy, my ego was taking a hit. But then I looked at Shane and saw how happy he was and was reminded why we started out on this CrossFit journey to begin with—so I could create great "See what you can do with your life" stories for my future children. But now, with my daughter Willow, that intangible why has turned into a reality. So that purpose now shifts to the present. I wouldn't need to tell stories to my children; they will be able to experience them in real time because I'll be getting back on the floor soon enough. That thought sparked an entirely new level of excitement to get back out there.

Being okay with the body changing. It's funny, I didn't start to show until quite late. As my belly began to expand and my boobs got bigger, I was faced with my body changing once again. In the past, it changed because of the training; this time it was adapting to support a growing baby. It was a shock at first; I had just spent years dedicating my life to sculpting my body in a way that allows me to perform at my absolute best, and now for the first time in my life I had to be okay with excess weight to support the baby. Even though I put on weight for bobsled or weight lifting, that was mostly muscle. This was fat with cellulite and stretch marks. It took some time, but I shifted my thinking and now revel in how remarkable the body is and what it is capable of.

I don't know what my future holds when it comes to being a mum. I just know I will try to be the best mum in the world. One thing is for sure: I have a new why and I'm eager to give it my best go.

Do Compare Yourself to Yourself

Beyond appearances, it is hard not to compare yourself with others. What do I do when such a thought gets me spiraling? I think back to where I started: where I was last week, where I was last month. I remind myself of the work I have done and the progress I've made. I compare myself only to myself. In 2021, Sydney Wells, an aspiring athlete and sister of Brooke Wells, worked tirelessly with Shane and the PRVN Fitness team to qualify for the semifinals during the 2021 CrossFit season. It was an amazing finish for such a new competitor. But then as the 2022 season rolled around, she tensed up and started to put too much pressure on herself, comparing herself to other competitors. I tried to help her see that she was piling on too many expectations.

"Sydney, remember where you were this time last year— you just learned how to do ring muscle-ups! And now you're doing three and stringing them together in a workout. Look at your progress! Don't be impatient. Be realistic about where you are. And don't compare yourself to your competition." I added, jokingly, "Take me, for example, I've been competing at this for eight years. And you've only done it for 12 months. Give the process some credit, as well as yourself." I tried to help her see it from a different point of view, and when I put it like that, we both laughed, but she got what I was trying to say. She was able to take a step back and reflect on where she was within the process of her development, without putting so much pressure on herself. It is a very easy trap for athletes—especially ones who are just beginning—to fall into. They put this external pressure on themselves by listening to the news media, commentators, social media, and all their friends and family.

I pride myself on being able to embrace this pressure and turn it into an advantage. Some seasons have been better than others, but even when I was just starting out, I was able to channel all that pressure from external outlets into motivation.

Embrace Your Differences

The beauty of CrossFit is that it's very broad—you need to be great at so many components of fitness, 10 to be exact: cardiovascular/respiratory, endurance, stamina, strength, flexibility, power, coordination, agility, balance, and accuracy. Since I am one of the smaller athletes on the field, I've made it my mission to be the strongest out there. I make up for my smallness with power and brute strength—and do what I can to beat the taller, bigger women. Inevitably, the bigger athletes will sometimes say they can't do all the body-weight movements as efficiently as I can because they are heavier. The smaller athletes say they don't have the body weight behind them to lift as much as the heavier athletes. You are always going to have an advantage in one or more things—and a disadvantage in one or more things. Don't feel sorry for yourself—embrace those differences and make sure you take advantage of your best assets and minimize the downsides. I get it—I'm small. I can't undo that fact. But I don't use it as an excuse not to do something—I use it to become the best in everything else. Something that I live by: I don't see my smallness as a weakness. There will always be things that I need to improve on, but I don't look at them as limitations, because if you look at them that way, you're telling yourself that you're not good at something. That's a defeatist argument. You should believe that you're good at everything you do.

You can always improve on things, of course, but be careful about slipping into perfectionism. There is a saying, "Perfect is the enemy of the good," and it is true. Perfect is not attainable, but just do the best you can every day. Case in point: In early summer 2021, I had gotten to where I was crushing all of my PRs every day in training, leading into the Games. I was checking all my goals off my list. And I still felt restless, unsatisfied. We were in our car, driving home from our gym, when I shared my frustration with Shane.

"I feel like my numbers could be even better. How can I get even better?"

Shane detected a hint of irritation in my words.

"Why aren't you happy?"

"I know I can do more. I want *more*."

"Tia, you need to take a step back and you need to understand that you have to appreciate these moments. Always trying to achieve or excel and be perfect is just plain unrealistic. Don't get me wrong, you can constantly strive for greatness, but being perfect is just not maintainable. And while you see frustration, I see growth."

He was right: There's a fine line between striving to be unstoppable and striving to be perfect. If you try to be perfect, you will constantly disappoint yourself because perfection is unattainable. This concept is hard for me as I have always been my harshest critic. But it was one of the best pieces of advice he has ever given me.

Food for Thought

All this is to say that the standard of the female ideal, especially in athletics, is impossible to attain. Even though there is increased awareness, women battle body-image issues throughout their careers—some of which can become outright dangerous. Whether it is pressure they put on themselves or pressure from outside sources, women may succumb to this pressure and risk developing a host of mental health issues and eating disorders that can plague their lives forever. These two topics are far too weighty for me to adequately cover in this book—but I want to address them briefly because, while I haven't gone through this or had anyone close to me battle such issues, I do know they exist. It is easy to get caught up in that impossible female standard of beauty, so to keep up appearances they keep their caloric intake down to avoid looking bloated or softening those six-pack abs. Calorie restriction can degenerate into issues like bulimia and anorexia. Blurring the lines even further is the constant gratification they get from social media, with comments like, "Oh, your abs are amazing. . . . You look so hot. . . ." They then take on that image of what others perceive them to be, and they feel they must hold on to that image, even to the detriment of their performance—and in the long run, their health.

If you are battling anxiety, depression, or eating issues, the best thing you can do is ask for help. It's okay to reach out to people who have had experience in this department. Talking about and understanding what you are going through can always help you overcome it and walk away stronger for it. It's not shameful, as there are so many people who go through similar struggles—knowing you are not alone is half the battle.

The Takeaway

If there is anything I can offer you today it's this: I so appreciated my journey to body positivity—it has taught me a lot about self-esteem and confidence, and I don't think I could stand in the position I do today if I hadn't learned to accept my body, both in its strength and its appearance. I am a lot more self-assured when talking to people—I don't care about what they think of me nearly as much as I did before I started Cross-Fit. If you are just starting out, you may be seeing a little bit more muscle popping up in places you didn't expect—my traps were the first development in my muscle growth. Take a deep breath and embrace the beauty in the strength you are discovering in your own body. I am so proud of the way my body looks because I know what I have done to get here. And I dare that boy in the third grade to disagree!

CHAPTER 7

Don't Call It a Comeback

Overcoming Setbacks and Getting Back Out There

Pop. *Whoa, what was that?* I had been killing it in my back squats when I felt something shift on the lower right side of my back. I stood up, thinking that would help with whatever the heck was going on, but the pain only got sharper—it was as if a dagger had been driven into my back.

It was 2014, I was about to turn 21, and I had just started weight training in hopes of making it to the Olympics (as well as leveling up my CrossFit). An athlete always has an overwhelming sense that they don't have much time to qualify, and this was certainly the case here. So training was intense and overlapped with my other priorities.

I can admit now that I did take training to an extreme, as I was obsessed with the possibility of representing my country on the world stage. As a little girl, I always dreamed of going to the Olympics, so you can only imagine the determination and the drive that I brought to my training, and I wasn't going to let anything stand in my way. It wasn't easy, as weight lifting was a whole new world for me. It took me several months to learn the fundamentals of the sport, but all of it ignited a fire within me. I wanted to challenge myself and see how much better I could get. So when I felt that pop in my back, I only had myself to blame for what happened next. Instead of putting my ego aside and reminding myself how important it was to listen to my body, I kept squatting, trying my hardest to pretend that nothing had happened. I also didn't want to take the easy way out—I was adamant about pushing through the pain. I didn't tell anyone and kept going because I was so scared that someone would tell me I had to stop. I didn't want anyone holding me back from going to the Olympics, and I also mistakenly thought I'd be fine: I just needed to sleep the pain off.

So I took a (singular) day off, but then went on to "train through the pain." Little did I know I had caused a hairline fracture and a compressed and bruised bone in my vertebrae.

I competed at the CrossFit Regionals soon after, and I could barely walk off the floor after one event—it was strict handstands/push-ups/burpees over the bar and front squats. I should have stopped with the amount of pain I was in, but I pushed through it. At the time, I just felt like I needed to keep proving that I had what it takes, and, besides, one day my back would just get better—right?

After seven months of working through the pain, I had had

enough. I had to tell Shane. I had been so stubborn because I didn't want to be seen as "weak," but I could tell he had started noticing my discomfort. Every time I moved I would take extra care, as if I were going in slow motion. I even changed how I moved to work around the pain. But what pushed me over the line was one day when I couldn't even pick up a pair of socks on the floor without my back screaming back at me. I thought, *How am I going to pick up a barbell if I can't pick up some dang socks off the floor?* I had all these dreams and aspirations—but at this moment I could clearly see that those were getting further and further away from me, unless I did something about the injury.

"Tia, this isn't normal. You shouldn't be in so much pain. Let's get it checked out," Shane smartly suggested after I filled him in. We were living in a pretty rural area at this time, so we needed to take a six-hour drive to Brisbane to see a specialist.

"How long have you been suffering?" the doctor asked me while looking at the scan of my back.

"Seven months."

"Well, I hate to say it, but you have a hairline fracture. If you had come in for a scan immediately after the injury, all of that pain and the severity of the injury may have been avoided. Who knows where you would be right now? But I can guarantee you wouldn't be sitting here in this much agony and with this severe an injury."

Instead, it was six months of *no* physical activity—ouch. I lost more than a year to a problem that could have had a much easier resolution. This was a bit of a kick in the teeth. Not only had I let myself down, but I had let Shane down. I had let my coach down. I felt like I had let my gym as well as my training buddies down. Not only had I been lying to myself, but I'd been lying to the people I cared about, and that was something that, even now, as I write this, I recognize was just such an immature and silly decision. I let my ego get the better of me, and it cost me six months of doing nothing. No physical activity as I slowly—very slowly—let my back rest and recover.

The Goldilocks Rule for Setbacks

We all go through setbacks, challenges, obstacles . . . whatever you call what got in your way of achieving something great. You can't go through life without having them—or else you aren't really living. To get through them, you have to have the right mentality to power through. Whether it's a physical injury, a poor outcome in an important competition, or even something more personal, like a divorce or the loss of a loved one, you have to have that same mentality if you want to overcome them. Setbacks will happen, but they only have to set you back temporarily rather than totally derailing you.

The way I see it, there are three ways people can handle setbacks, with only one of them being the right way. The first is to ignore them (as I did). Wrong. The second way some people deal with setbacks is to dwell on the problem, wallowing in their misfortune or even blaming others for it. Also wrong. I have seen talented athletes, who feel they are not getting anywhere in their career, move from coach to coach as if that's going to rectify the problem. (It usually doesn't.) Others can use an injury as an excuse not to get back into training after proper recovery time.

In both situations, you will pay a heavy price, and you may never get over it. You see this in everyday life, too, not just in training or competition. The third option, what I call the Goldilocks Rule of Setbacks, is that sweet spot residing somewhere in the middle. In order to get over any challenge, you need to acknowledge it and take ownership of it. Otherwise, you may always feel like the victim and not be able to move on. Take time to recognize what the issue is and stop it from escalating. Learn from it and takes steps to move forward. Don't bury it and certainly don't wallow in it. You will never see the other side of it.

HOW TO BE RESILIENT WHEN A SETBACK HITS

1. **Acknowledge it.** I now know that in order to get over my back pain, I needed to first acknowledge it. We first need to admit to ourselves that something is negatively impacting our lives. Whether it is a family issue or a work issue, financial woes, or physical injury, we have to accept that something troubling is going on. We can't hide it. We can't bury the problem, as it will only get bigger with time. I made a huge mistake in not admitting that I had to slow down and take a break. Instead, I created a

ripple effect that cost me more time and pain than it should have, not to mention other people's time as well. I had put my health in jeopardy and I didn't do what my body deserved. We all have bad days, and we need to acknowledge and work through it; ignoring it will ultimately make you lose out on the goals and aspirations that you wanted to go out and achieve. By accepting the problem, you will allow yourself time to pause, breathe, and regroup. And remember: You can only have a setback if you are trying to move forward in life. Think of a bow and arrow: To go forward, the arrow needs to be drawn backward. Sometimes you have to move backward to move forward. But it is all good—going backward first to progress forward is so much better than staying stuck in one place.

2. **Learn from it and build resilience.** Ultra-marathoner Scott Jurek once said, "Injuries are the best teachers." It doesn't have to be a physical injury to teach us that living means we are not free of pain or loss, but it's what we do with it that proves our mettle. You're always going to face adversity; you're always going to face challenges. How you address those situations—not just as an athlete, but as a human being—will help you adapt. You can't change the past, but you can *be present* in the present so you can better your future. Without challenge, you don't change.

3. **Take a long-term view on rising above it.** Keep everything in perspective. Whether you want to lose weight, perform at your best, or get a new job, it is up to you to make it happen. It may take time. Focus on what you can control. If you stick to a deliberate approach, you'll have a "Setbacks will come, but they won't break you"

attitude to keep you going. Aim for small improvements. Step by step, day by day, moment by moment, you'll soon find that you've made big progress. You never want to become too overwhelmed with the work yet to come.

4. **Plan for your return.** If you haven't quite reached your goal yet, accept that you may have fallen short of your goal this time. But that doesn't mean you won't ever accomplish it, no matter how small it is. I will fail in a movement one day, but the next I will go in even more determined to hit it, and, boom, I get it. As long as I don't give up, I know I will keep trying until I achieve it. Take my bobsledding dream—it didn't play out the way I had pictured it, but that doesn't mean I was defined by the outcome of that experience. If I look back at all my progress from where I began, compared to where I finished at the end of the season, my technique, strength, and speed improved tremendously.

Get Back Out There

Whenever there is a setback or you have fallen short of a goal, you sometimes need to take a break, as I did. The next step after taking a break and working on your resilience is getting back out there. Sometimes that can be as frightening as the setback itself. Here are some go-to tips to getting back on track.

Don't think too much. Don't think about how much you have to do, how far you have to go, what challenges you have to face to get things back on track. Just take one day at a time, one moment at a time. As I said earlier, don't overwhelm yourself with what's to come or what has happened in the past. Be present where you are now. Seriously, don't think and just let your subconscious take over. You'll read more about this in chapter 9, but I've done this for so many years now that I have become quite good at not thinking and just allowing my body to do what it is supposed to do. Don't worry: Your body will remember, as it has muscle memory. When I have been off all year, sometimes I start thinking, *Oh man, I've forgotten how to snatch—can I do this anymore?* It takes me one to two weeks to get back to where I was, but I always do. And every year I go through that process every single time because I've had to take the necessary break to let the mind and body rest, recover, reset, and recharge. And then I start over.

When I'm in that process of getting back into training, I can start to think, *This. Is. So. Hard.* It is hard because the last time I was there in the gym I was at my peak, and then the next time, after I've had some time off, I'm back at zero. It can be hard to face. And you have a really high mountain to climb. So I try to keep myself in the present moment and just focus on the here and now. That allows me to overcome that doubt and to feel that everything is going to be okay and just embrace the process once again. *Cool. That was a win because I got through it.* And I'll take those little wins as they come. This thinking can be for anyone in any sort of situation, not just in sports. Trust in the process and you know you will be ready when the time is right.

Get over the first-week (or first-day, or first-hour) hump. When I have been away from training, I say to myself, *Let's get through the first day.* And when I see that I can push through the first week, then I know that I'm on the right track. By the second week, I've found that rhythm again. So just brave it for the first few days; it's all about that initial block that you have to overcome. And I think that's always the hardest because you know in your head how far you have to go.

It can be hard to find the motivation, and even then, it can come and go, but if you stick to the road map, take it day by day, you'll get there. Then one day—usually when you least expect it—you will finally feel that you're progressing and getting better, another reason you should always show up to your training. I know when I hit that moment: The weights feel really good in my hands, my movements feel smooth and efficient, and my lungs embrace my quick breathing.

Take your time. I have a habit of always wanting to push, push, push, but it actually put me in more of a deficit when I was trying to heal. Sometimes giving your all 100 percent of the time is actually not optimal, especially if you're recovering from an injury.

If you have an injury and you push through, you are not training at your best because the injury is limiting you in some capacity. I'd say it's more like 60–75 percent of your best, and I'd doubt you are getting any benefits. Instead, Shane suggests resting for up to a week—no training at all. Let's say you have a shoulder injury—you're limited in what you can do with that shoulder. If you train around that injury, you could extend the injury a week to two weeks or even longer. It's better to rest the shoulder for a few days—that way you will find yourself back in form and training at your typical pace sooner than later. You can train—just concentrate on the opposite part of the body when doing so. For instance, if I have an arm injury, I do only lower-body work; if I have a knee injury, I'll do an upper-body session for a few days. It's common to think that we need to push through it, because it sucks to miss out on days of training. But what's actually happening when you average it out, your performance ranges from 60 percent to 70 percent, over the course of two or three weeks. You're still better off having two days of 0 percent and then being back to 100 percent. (And, of course, always consult a doctor if your injury is more severe or does not get better.)

Today, I'm so in tune with my body that I know the recovery protocols I need to do to loosen my lower back so I don't ever get to that point. And, if I had never learned from that experience, I would have continued to just keep pushing through pain because I thought that going hard all the time was always the best thing. It may come as a shock, but I am not required to produce 100 percent output in every session. It took me a long time to learn this, but the major upside to this has allowed for more cognitive thinking about movement patterns and body positions rather than "blacking out" and going numb in workouts. We couldn't maintain 100 percent every single day. I probably train 90–95 percent of my true capacity in comparison to competition. We will do workouts where I'm pulling off 100 percent or even 120 percent, just so I know that I have the ability to go there in competition, but it's like a marathon. When you train for a marathon, you never do the full 26.2 miles until race day. There is a time and place and that's when I rely on Shane to tell me when to go there and when to slow down a bit.

I will admit that there are times I find myself becoming impatient. For example, throughout the 2022 season, I felt like I had to play catchup after taking time off and focusing on the bobsled. I found myself falling into the trap of overdoing it in training. (I mean, really, I should listen to my own advice!) Because I pushed myself too much, I reinjured my back, which put me in the worst position for an athlete: the possibility of not being able to compete at the pinnacle of your sporting career. I knew I was getting significantly better than my previous self in the 2021 season; however, the extra strain I put on myself made me tired and I fell into the trap of not allowing myself to rest and recover. I was taking on too much outside the gym, and I was running out of time to fit in my recovery and rest. It was only fitting that the back pain returned. But I muddled through and won, reclaiming my seat.

Don't call it a comeback. In August 2018, after giving birth to her daughter a year earlier, Serena Williams appeared in a Chase Bank ad promoting the US Open. It starts with an intimate moment with her baby before she starts on a workout, all while she is reciting the lyrics to LL Cool J's "Mama Said Knock You Out" with the line: "Don't call it a comeback. I've been here for years I'm rocking my peers. Puttin' suckers in fear." In her Instagram post that accompanied the ad, she wrote: "Lots of people have called this my 'comeback.' But becoming a mom isn't something I'm coming back from. It's part of who I am. It's been both incredibly amazing and incredibly tough, but it's only made me stronger."

What a great attitude to have! This spoke to me when the ad first aired, but it means more now because I can relate—the fire within me to compete only grew when I got pregnant. No matter what goes on in your life, you are not making a comeback—there is nothing to come back from when you are a champion.

Have a role model. British tennis champion Andy Murray has long been an underdog in his field. Persistent hip issues and other physical challenges have plagued him throughout his career, but he always kept fighting. I really admire the fierce persistence, in his pursuit of his craft and his passion. I was always curious to know what drove him. What made him feel so hungry to keep showing up and roll with the punches? His grit and resilience can be so much more inspiring than the seemingly effortless triumphs of the winning athlete. If he can do it, so can I.

Bethany Hamilton is another one. A world-class surfer, she was already surfing by the age of 7. In 2003, when she was only 13, she survived a terrifying shark attack in which she lost her left arm. Even though many said it couldn't be done, she got back on the surfboard—and did so within a month of the injury. Today she is considered one of the top surfers in the world. Talk about determination. Find a role model or a good friend who can inspire you to carry on as you get back in fighting form.

Advice for Mini-Setbacks

When my back was reinjured right before the 2022 Games, it got so bad that Shane, my family, and I were worried I wouldn't be able to compete. I knew, however, that if I could physically move, I would compete. As my back got gradually worse, I started to get more panicky. *Not again*, I thought. The difference this time was that I knew how to handle it, and I was more mature, more experienced. I thought I could hang on until after the Games, when I would finally be able to rest and recover. But I still had three weeks until the Games and it wasn't the right time to start tapering. That Sunday, I couldn't get myself out of bed without pain. I couldn't even pick my knees up high enough to do a warm-up jog around the track for our morning session. I walked off the track saying nothing, but my eyes were filled with tears. My dad followed me—he knew something was up. I knew I needed to figure out a solution, and it was comforting to have my parents in town so Shane could stay focused on the other PRVN athletes. We decided that I would take the next day off training, which *killed* me on the inside, but I had to reassure myself that I'd be getting more out of resting than putting my back under more strain. That day turned into a week, but it was the only way to ensure that I could move enough to compete. I was still in pain, but at least I could move efficiently with the pain.

You might be wondering as you read this: Hey, Tia, how come you didn't take your own advice and take time off to heal? Good question. But since I had been through this pain before, I knew my tolerance threshold. Even though it was a hard decision, I felt in my gut I could hold on for the Games and knew I could rest after the Games were over. I took advantage of any and all treatments available to keep the pain at a manageable level. Mum started to make up her concoctions (as Dad and I like to call them), comprising natural herbs and anti-inflammatories, which included turmeric, blueberries, bone broth, and anything else she believed would help me. Dad gave me massages to try to help loosen my hips in hopes that they would ease the tension. We even drove to a local sporting goods store to purchase an inversion table to help take the pressure off my lower back. (Desperate times call for desperate measures, but FYI, it didn't help much.) I also tried a litany of other treatments: cryotherapy, isolated cryotherapy, sauna and ice-bath contrasting, massage, acupuncture, NormaTec technology, and stretching. The real lifesaver was Devon, a body coach who works for TB12 (a company owned by Tom Brady and his lifelong personal trainer, Alex). He gave me treatments all day, every day, so my preparation for the

CrossFit Games looked very different from a typical lead-up to the competition (instead of training, I lay on the bed, allowing Devon to give me excruciatingly deep massages). Devon continued giving me treatments throughout the Games. Each day he'd loosen up my hips and lower back in order to get me to move again. I still had pain, but I could physically move, which was what I needed to compete. The trick was to activate the muscle groups around my back and release the tendons and muscle groups that were overworking and not firing. The evening treatment was as grueling and agonizing, but Devon would do his best to align and reset my back. Some may agree or disagree with this aggressive type of treatment, but I was determined that nothing was going to get in my way of walking onto the competition floor to *win*.

This is a good example of what I call mini-setbacks. These are things that happen in either the lead-up to a competition or in the middle of it. Either way, you need to make a decision quickly in the moment or you may make a mistake or lose time. You may get overwhelmed and start losing your cool. When this happens, you need to take that time to recenter yourself, because the more you get overwhelmed, the more you may dig yourself into a hole.

And even though I was able to compete, I was still in my own hole at the 2022 Games.

That first day, the Games started with a bang, but not as big a bang as I would have liked: I came in second in the bike event. *That's okay, but I can do better*, I thought. The next workout (after a rain delay) was where I messed up and, in my eyes, it was uncharacteristic. The event that started with jump ropes took me to unfamiliar territory: One of the requirements in this first movement was to perform all 75 single jumps, unbroken, before you can progress. So, if you get to 74 and make a mistake, you have to start all over again. I got to 40 and I messed up, so I started thinking, *Don't mess up again, don't mess up.* I had been very confident going into this workout because they were movements that we had practiced in training on a regular basis, so 75 unbroken was going to be easy. That's where I was wrong. I got comfortable and switched off, and, in a way, I disrespected the movement by thinking this would be easy. It resulted in a costly mistake. There was zero time to worry about it; all I could do was make up as much time as possible to ensure that I got into the next heat. My immediate thought was, *Come on Tia. You're better than this. Relax but concentrate. Make up the time that you have lost. Smooth reps are fast reps.* The trick was not to rush the movements and make more mistakes, but to catch up to the women in my heat and hope that it was enough to get into the next part of the workout. After I had crossed the finish line, I knew I had messed up. My fingers were crossed that I had made up enough time, though.

In the end, instead of doing the total of 75 single jumps, I had to do 125 because of the setbacks. I raced through the rest of the workout, but it didn't help. I wasn't fast enough. I placed terribly for my expectations—I finished 23rd and was eliminated from this event (you had to be in the top 20 to move forward). In the past few years, I hadn't placed higher than 6th in a workout, so not to progress to the next stage, not to mention not completing a workout, was unacceptable for the high expectations I had set for myself. It crossed my mind that my worrying about my back was keeping me from going full throttle. It was challenging not to dwell on this outcome, especially since I had to stand on the sidelines and watch my competition continue with the workout, but that is competition. It doesn't always go your way. And I do believe this happened for a reason, because I was even more motivated to showcase my talent and resilience, even after having made a mistake, and proving that no one could beat me.

Admittedly, there are some days when I don't hit it perfectly, but I execute everything to the best of my ability. But not with this workout. I made a huge mistake and it was definitely out of character for me. I never make these kinds of mistakes. I felt I wasn't in control, focusing on the missteps I was making versus the job at hand. Ultimately, I knew not to give much thought to my placing, because it was only the second workout of the weekend. I had potentially 10 more workouts to make up for it—plenty of time to catch up. What scared me was that I always do well, and this hiccup was not normal. Everyone thought I was finished. I could see the headlines being written. "CrossFit readies for the next generation of champions," and I used that to get me fired up. I thought, *Don't step in my way people, because I will rip you down.* I was only getting started! My mission at that moment was to remind them all that they're just competing for second, not first.

I was determined to turn everything around, so when the third event came up that day (with dips) I wanted so badly to regain control of the competition and put an end to the talk of people potentially beating me. I pushed my body to its limits—and didn't place very high once again, ninth. *What was happening?!* But this second hiccup truly ignited a fire in me that had been missing at the start of competition. I have a lot of respect for my peers, but I get very protective of my title, and when I think of them getting even a hint of hope that the crown is theirs for the taking, I kick into attack mode. I make it very clear how far they have to go to come anywhere near me. I also don't like having commentators trying to create controversy over who is going to threaten my title. There shouldn't be any talk of this.

After my fourth event—shoulder to overhead and shuttle runs—I ended that conversation.

CHAPTER 8

Complacency Is a Killer

Learn to Love the Pain and Never Be Satisfied

So much of what goes on in CrossFit is preparing for the unknown—and that is the beauty of the sport. Unlike traditional sports, in which athletes know what they are getting into before competition—a skier prepares for a downhill or slalom race, a runner trains for a marathon or a 400m sprint—the events in the CrossFit Games are, for the most part, announced only a few hours/days before the event. The Games might include swimming, running, bike riding, weight lifting and power lifting movements, gymnastics, strongman movements, paddleboarding—and they might not. You might have trained really hard all season on your rope climbs or dumbbell snatches, but, come Games week, those movements aren't in there. The idea behind this is that the fittest athletes should be able to handle anything that comes their way. With every Games different, you have to prepare for anything and everything. Welcome to CrossFit.

With nothing being a given in CrossFit, what *should* be a given is you. When you just focus on the task at hand and what is under your control, it allows you to truly let go and compete on your own time because you're not worried or wasting energy on what other people are doing. When you focus on what you—and only you—can control, then you are present in that moment; you don't allow external things to affect your judgment or your performance. This principle proves out even more in daily life, too, because no one knows what their future holds. No one is ever immune to struggles in life, so you need to evolve and adapt. It all comes back to focusing on you, being comfortable with the unknown and unknowable, and, most of all, not getting complacent.

Get Comfortable with the Uncomfortable

It is just part of human nature to gravitate to things within our comfort zone rather than push through things we don't feel comfortable with. But we know that doesn't get us anywhere in life, and in CrossFit, as a training methodology, it is all about getting comfortable with the uncomfortable. You never know what will be thrown at you, so every move, every muscle-up, every squat is about pushing yourself further, harder, deeper. I was always told that the better you become, the easier it will get. And it wasn't until three years into this CrossFit experience that I realized that's not the case at all.

It is so bloody hard.

But it is so satisfying at the same time because, when I look back on the journey, I can see how far I have come, and I can see the self-development I have made as an athlete. If I were to do a workout today at the level of difficulty I performed when I first started working out, it would be easy, because I've evolved so much and pushed my limits. That is the case for any athlete in any sport. But, as you improve, you need to make sure you keep leveling it up to keep it challenging. For example, there's a workout called Fran: It comprises 21 thrusters and 21 pull-ups, then 15 thrusters and 15 pull-ups, then 9 thrusters and 9 pull-ups, for time (meaning, as fast as possible). When I first started CrossFit, I would do this workout in four minutes. Now I can complete it in an under–two-minute time. Because I've gotten fitter, I've become more efficient. Because I've pushed through those boundaries and overcome the difficulty so many times, I know what I'm truly capable of. What was completely uncomfortable at first became doable. Same for dead lifts: At first, I would have struggled with 198-pound weights, but now I can lift 400 pounds. Keep in mind that this is over a 10-year progression, and now that I can do an under–two-minute Fran workout and 400-pound dead lift doesn't mean I am satisfied with those numbers—I'll keep pushing to better my PR on everything every day.

Change doesn't happen overnight, but improvement does come, and, with time, you will be amazed by the changes in your body. But you have to keep pushing through what's uncomfortable, making your body go where it doesn't want to go. One trick I have used to embrace the uncomfortable is to "flip the script." If I don't like doing something, I will turn it around and learn to love it. When a movement or workout is especially hard for me, I will embrace it rather than avoid it. I do so because it helps me push through, and I know my struggle to complete it will, in the end, make me that much better, stronger, faster. It's funny, people will often ask me whether I have a favorite movement or a movement I hate—but I tell them I like all the movements equally, much as a mother loves all their children equally. They may be all different and some may be more challenging than others, but I love them all the same.

Why do I do this? Well, if you look at squats and think, *I hate squatting*, that's where you create that mentality of struggle, and you set yourself up for failure. You don't allow yourself to enjoy it as long as you've labeled it as something you don't like. Don't get me wrong: I'm human—there are always going to be harder elements of a workout, but you can't go into it dreading it, or you will naturally psych yourself out of it. Rather, psych yourself into it by thinking how good you will feel when you're done, knowing that you pushed through it. The more you do this, the more you will change your mindset and it will feel less and less like a struggle.

For sure, there are some movements I will always find tough due to simple body mechanics. For instance, a Rogue Echo bike is harder for me than it is for Brooke Wells, who is much taller than me and has really long legs. Those with longer limbs typically can move that machine a lot faster and a lot more efficiently than athletes with shorter legs. But I never want biology to be an excuse. While I'll recognize that a taller athlete will be better at the bike, when it comes to air squats, I have the edge since I am more compact and my range of motion is much smaller. I can do more in the time limit and outpace my taller competitors. The same goes for body weight: There aren't any body-weight categories in the sport of CrossFit—some would say this is unfair, but it all plays out evenly in the end. The athletes who have less body weight will most likely perform better doing gymnastics/body-weight movements and the larger athletes will most likely perform better in the weight-lifting/odd object movements.

Those around you need to be on board with this mentality. For Shane, as my coach, it's crucial how he uses his words. If he said, "Oh, Tia, you're going to struggle with this movement," he would be setting me up for failure. Take the pegboards back in the 2015 Games—it was a movement I had never done before, but he gave me the confidence to leave no doubt by reframing my thought process. Here is what I mean: When I was climbing the pegboards, rather than Shane saying to me, "DON'T let go!" he encouraged me to "Hold on!" They both mean the same thing, but one is more positive than the other, and your brain definitely picks up on the subtlety of positivity rather than negativity.

Embrace the Pain

I will admit, on the other hand, that I just don't like training, period. It *hurts* and it's *so hard*. But it's a critical part of the process, and I can't compete without it. So I embrace it, knowing that every day I'm constantly getting better at whatever I put my mind to. For instance, muscle-ups were tough for me, but after constant training, breaking down the movement, and doing weighted muscle-ups, strict muscle-ups, double dip muscle-ups, tempo muscle-ups, and the 100 variations of mixed workouts that include muscle-ups, I've become very good at them. To get better, you need to accept the pain and the struggle that come with it. I embrace every ounce of blood, sweat, and tears. Pain never goes away, but if you have your why clearly in your head, it's always going to be manageable.

As with every workout, there is a level of challenge that goes with it. You're faced with the question: Do I keep going and push through this wall or do I stop and take a break? Do I quit or keep pushing forward and embrace the hurt and the pain that comes with a workout? My answer: Keep going—even as your body screams at you for doing so. I love it when people ask me what I do for a living and I say, "I'm an athlete. I train full time." They respond, "Oh, how lucky are you to go to the gym and just work out all day." If they only knew what it really takes to be at the gym all day every day. I am *training*, not exercising—there is definitely a difference between the two.

Life Lessons

Often, you are faced with situations that bring a level of frustration, pain, and headache, where you have to ask yourself: Am I going to embrace this or am I going to look the other way? And if you do look away, you'd be avoiding the reality of your problems rather than overcoming them. Whenever I'm in this sort of situation, I try to apply my training wisdom of pushing forward and embracing the suck—until I get the job done.

Otherwise, I have always found that if you quit once, it's that much easier to quit a second time and a third. It just keeps getting easier not to face your problems head-on. It's when the excuses come out and people list reasons why they haven't accomplished their goals—or maybe why they are too scared to even try to reach their goals. They never take ownership and lie to themselves about what the real problem may be and play victim. Pain and challenges are always going to try to shake you off balance in life, but you can't let that happen.

If I feel that I am about to explode, I ask myself, *How badly do I want this? More than anything in the world!* I answer my own question. And I continue. I learned a lot about maximizing my pain threshold from Josh Bridges. In 2015, when I met him and trained with him in the lead-up to the Games, I thought if I could have only a quarter of his intensity and stamina, I'd be in kick-ass shape for the Games. At our last training session, Josh told me a story that forever stuck with me.

"During my Navy SEAL days, my commander would always ask during exercises, 'How is the pain?' and we'd all reply, 'It hurts, sir.'

"The captain would then say, 'GOOD! Is it hard?'

" 'Yes, sir!' " we'd all reply.

" 'GOOD!' "

This story also stuck with Josh: He has the word GOOD written on posterboard up on the wall in his garage where he trained daily. Whenever a slight trace of doubt threatened to creep in, he would look at that poster and remind himself, "This pain is GOOD. It's making me stronger, fitter, faster. I need this in order to be better. If other people can do it, so can I."

This practice stuck with me and it helped me get through some of the not-so-high points of my workouts. Whenever I was in pain, I reassured myself, This is GOOD. This is what makes a champion. I embraced it because, just like Josh, I wanted to get better and I wanted to see how good I could be and that is why I push myself to my limits EVERY SINGLE DAY.

It's a mentality I have to practice on a daily basis. I have to constantly remind myself that I want this. Over the many years that I've been doing this, I realize that it's how you embrace the pain that dictates whether or not you can move forward and overcome any obstacle. Because the thing is, I don't feel any less pain than you feel when you go into the gym. My drive and my determination allow me to accept it more than any other person. Say, for example, someone's going through a really hard time in their life—maybe they lost their job. That person is obviously going to go through a lot of pain. They'll inevitably ask a lot of questions: Where was that turning point that led me down this path? Did I do something to deserve this? Why me? But you don't want to belabor why something went wrong or why this situation has happened; what you *can* do is understand it and look forward. What can you learn from it? How can you evolve from this? What do you need to do to overcome this?

Pain Is Not Always Physical

In 2021, Shane added several new employees at our PRVN business to help us take on more athletes to train and to work with the trainers and continue to coach. He was getting pulled in several different directions every moment of the day. Plus, he has me, and I constantly demand his attention (because that is what I do and at the end of the day, I am his wife, it's my job, right?!), and that adds a lot more pressure on him.

Looking back on it now, I can only imagine the level of pressure and uncertainty that must have been building inside him. Shane tends not to dwell on the small things and can stay detached emotionally, but it couldn't have been an easy time for him. (I'm not sure if that's a male thing, but I have found that the men in my life do a very good job of stripping emotion out of every situation.) Shane never said anything, but I couldn't help but be overwhelmed for him by how much he was juggling and how hard he was being pulled in the different directions. I felt helpless and frustrated, and, as his wife, I felt his pain. It was all just part of the growing pains of expanding our brand.

All of this goes back to the concept of embracing the pain—they don't call it "growing pains" because it is pleasant. It is something that you have to go through every single day of your life outside of the gym. And it doesn't matter who you are or what you've done. Everyone goes through something tough; you always have to face adversity, and you always have to go through challenges and obstacles in order to grow. Building good, strong habits on how you overcome these obstacles helps you apply them in different facets of life. It's the way you embrace those challenges that determines your fate. And because success comes in so many different forms, your true definition of success is probably different from mine. That's something that's really important to understand. Because in some people's eyes success is the amount of money they have in their bank accounts or investments they have in their name. But for me, success thus far has come from accomplishments and that makes me feel validated. Over the years of pursuing them, I have grown into a more confident, more open-minded, and stronger individual. I was successful in accomplishing my goal of making it to the Olympics or even placing second at my first CrossFit Games because I knew anything was possible and that gave me a sense of power. All the pain is worth it when it serves your why.

Never Be Satisfied

Many people, especially those in a high-performance environment, are constantly striving for greatness and trying to keep that extra edge. It's so true when people say, "It's hard to get to the top, but it's even harder to stay at the top." Never becoming complacent is a crucial part of staying there. NEVER BE SATISFIED.

I don't want anyone to mistake my aspiration to be undeniably the best in the world. I know, that's a pretty bold statement. Even as I write those words I can feel the butterflies fly in my belly because I can't help but think, *Oh, my gosh, when people read that, they're gonna think how cocky I am.* But it doesn't matter what other people think; it matters what I think, and since I want to be undeniable, there is not a lot of room for being okay with the status quo.

Throughout my journey, I have always had to juggle distractions and make sure that I had my priorities in order. I always asked myself at every turn and decision, *Is this my BEST effort?"* I wanted to ensure that every move I made wasn't a move toward complacency.

From 2015 to 2017, I owned and operated our own Cross-Fit affiliate back in Australia, where I had to juggle a lot while not jeopardizing my own competitive goals. At the Games, I had to attend to gym business and member requests while not allowing any stress to seep into my own performance. You would think this would be too much pressure—but this time period turned out to be the most motivating for me. I was still proving myself and had eyes on the prize, and this time I was not only representing myself, but also my business. If I did well, my business would reap the rewards since a gym being run by a CrossFit champion certainly has more cachet than one that doesn't. These three years proved I had all the hunger I needed to be on top of the podium at the CrossFit Games.

At the beginning of each season during this time, we would implement something new or change something up and make sure it fit and enhanced our competitiveness. These changes included moving to the United States and being more accessible to sponsors, which helped boost our income and financial support, incorporating training partners, and opening up our tiny little circle to allow for additional support and company in my training days. It also meant welcoming new relationships into our lives and saying goodbye to previous ones. These decisions were driven by one simple question: "Will this help contribute to standing on top of the podium?" All this was to ensure I was not becoming complacent.

I'm telling you now: Complacency—it's a killer.

I have watched too many businesspeople and athletes become complacent and lose their edge. I have been hypervigilant in not letting that happen to me. I'm definitely not perfect, and

I have come dangerously close to complacency as the years went on and I fell into a rhythm and routine. It's easy to become comfortable in your environment. So how do you keep it from happening? It's about recognizing those moments. I know Shane is so good at constantly questioning whether we are doing enough, not just in the gym and during training, but in life, in investing, and setting up our future in business and reaching our full potential. One of these questions allowed us to see that we were ready to open up our gym doors to other competitive athletes and have them train with us. We figured the shared interaction and training would help me level up and demand better from myself, which would help me steer clear of becoming complacent within my own performance and environment.

Don't Eat the Cheese

Let's say you achieve the level of success you have always wanted. You get to the top of the podium and all the accolades that come with it. You feel that you are on the top of the world—and now you can rest easy, right? It's hard to stay motivated when you feel like you accomplished what you set out to do. When you are feeling good about yourself, you may want to ease off the gas, but don't. Nope, now is the time to hit the gas. Take advantage of the momentum you have and don't be satisfied.

Famed Dallas Cowboys football coach Bill Parcells used to say, "Don't eat the cheese" to his team when they won a big game. What he meant was that while you can revel in success for a short time, don't start taking it for granted. Don't start buying into your own hype, and don't buy into what everybody tells you. In other words, don't be the mouse that eats the cheese in the trap.

How do you avoid this? First, by maintaining awareness. Check yourself and see if you may be falling into that trap of contentment (which leads to complacency). Second, set higher standards—big or small—to offset that complacency. One simple way I stay grounded is by doing daily chores, such as vacuuming and cleaning my house. Such mundane but necessary tasks keep my feet firmly planted on the ground. Being unstoppable means getting hungrier every time you win; understanding what you've accomplished just gives you the opportunity to do more. Remember to adjust your why so you are always moving toward a new goal if you've mastered your previous one.

Don't Let Others Make You Soft

While we can be our own worst enemies when it comes to complacency, I believe the company you keep can contribute to it as well. We discussed this concept earlier in the book, but the saying "You are who you surround yourself with" is so true. If you surround yourself with people who are content and live a simple, happy-go-lucky life, that is most likely the way you will live your life. (And that is okay, if that is how you want to live your life. But I am guessing that if you're reading my book, this is not you; you are trying to figure out how to either change your mindset or find that motivation to reach your full potential in life.) On the other hand, if you surround yourself with type A achievers who strive for greatness, their vision is contagious and you can't help but have similar aspirations.

When I embarked on my bobsled journey, I entered an environment that wasn't familiar to me. Shane and I always prided ourselves on our high standards of excellence, but we soon found ourselves with people who weren't embracing a championship mentality, and it was the first time I realized how important and powerful it was to surround yourself with like-minded people. While I was disappointed, I get it—sometimes people are still trying to figure out what they want—but I wasn't there to figure it out for them. I was there to win.

We worked doggedly with the team to change their mindset from just being there and participating to actually competing to win. In some people's minds, just being there is the accomplishment. That, to me, is complacency. Being there is only part of the process—giving 110 percent is winning. If more people had that mentality, they would probably shock themselves and realize that they would place better than they thought they could.

However, I do have to remember that winning is just a by-product of how I compete and all the hard work I devote to my craft. I will only think about it when I'm standing on top of the podium and when I'm looking for that why throughout the season when I need a bit of motivation to get me through a hard day of training. What I have to do now is get to work. And not get distracted. Or complacent. Or lazy.

KEEP COMPLACENCY AT BAY

1. Remember your why. And, as you now know, your why can change every year; it really depends on where you are in your life. It doesn't stay the same. Therefore, always asking yourself why you want to pursue a certain endeavor can keep you in check, keep you aligned with your end goal, and keep you from getting complacent.
2. Maintain a balance. Yes, be on autopilot (in the zone), but also be mindful that you want to push yourself as much as you can. It's so easy to take on too much without realizing it. So check in daily.
3. Keep focused so you can stay in the flow. Constantly coming back to your why and remembering what the end goal is will always help you keep that momentum going.

It's all about putting in more than you think you can, because to be at the top of your game, to be the greatest at your craft, you cannot sit back. You have to keep on being your best. You have to challenge yourself in ways others can't or won't. To stay on top of the mountain, you can't be satisfied. You have to keep moving forward and keep your foot on the gas. The late great Kobe Bryant was known to have said: "Rest at the end, not in the middle."

CHAPTER 9

Sharpen the Sword

No Thinking, Especially No Negative Thinking

It happens nearly every time I am about step out on the competition floor. My eyes tear up from excitement as I think to myself, *I'm about to blow the roof off this place.* It's my body's reaction to knowing what I'm capable of doing and what is about to happen. I am about to unleash, and it's because I am about to get in the zone. I have done the work and I am *so* ready.

When it matters, I can allow myself to turn off all the noise—of the crowd, of the commentators, of my own anxious voice in my head—and be completely present and confident that my preparation and training will take over.

While being *in the zone* may feel different for everyone, for me, when I am in it, I feel like I am in a relaxed, focused state. My mind is perfectly blank and I don't feel any pain. I don't feel any emotion. I've literally allowed my subconscious to take control. I'm still very focused, but every part of my body takes over. Even though I'm physically exerting a lot of energy, I couldn't be any more relaxed or any more in control. I don't get it every time in competition, but the more I do it, the more I can tap into the zone. And the more I compete, the more I feel it, and after a while it will feel like second nature. You will be amazed at how it can improve your performance. It drives me to compete again and again.

How can you get this? How can you up your game and start standing on top of the podium instead of watching others do it? Well, it is different for everyone, but here is my take on how I have been able to train myself to get in the zone.

First, it always goes back to doing the work. If you do enough of the training, your body and mind will be so conditioned that they will work for you. Having that self-assurance allows me to show up and win before I've even begun. And it will help you, too. Your muscle memory will kick in so you can turn your mind off and let your subconscious do the work. When you've trained so hard that you are truly present in the moment, you are untouchable. There's no better feeling than that.

Turn Off the Conscious Mind, Turn on the Subconscious Body

The time to ruminate and overthink is *not* in competition. Whatever thoughts you may have had coming into a game or tournament, they have no place while competing. Flip that switch off and go on autopilot. Get out of your own way to your success. If you are stressed or anxious, doubt will creep in and mess you up. You will never get in the zone.

When I go out on the floor, I just do what I did in training: I focus on one rep at a time, and I pay attention to every single movement. If it is with dumbbells, I think, *My right hand has the dumbbell and is going to go up over my head; I'm going to bring it to my shoulder.* Simple. *As I go up overhead, I'm going to step forward with my left foot. Then, I'm going to bring my feet back in line with each other. I'm going to repeat that, bring it to my left shoulder, and then step forward with my right foot, as my hand goes up overhead. I'm just going to keep repeating that.* And that's all I think about—the particular movement at the particular time. I don't think about who is in front of me; I don't think about my judge; I don't even hear the crowd. I stay in my lane. I continue: *I have one more rep to go. I'm going to put it down. I'm going to walk forward, then I'm going to run back and I'm going to go straight up onto the pegboard.* Every single moment is focused on every single movement until I cross that finish line. I just trust that my body knows what to do. I know I have done all the work and that I am fit enough; I know the movements enough; and there's nothing in my mind that makes me think or feel anything else but that present job at hand. It's not until I am giving a big loud roar as I cross the finish line that I realize how in the zone I was.

As I move along in the event, as everyone's falling and

dropping behind me, I'm finding that flow. Some had gone out too hard or didn't stick to their game plan, but I'm just continuing to focus on my task at hand. It has actually gotten to a point in our coaching relationship where Shane doesn't even need to tell me how to do things because he has trained me so well. I am in control but so free at the same time.

Stay in Control

While competing, I don't focus on the end result or who is in the lead. I try not to look at the leaderboard throughout competition. It doesn't matter what's going to happen, you're going to be lining up against your competitors anyway. When you start worrying about things out of your control, *you* will become out of control.

If you make a mistake, remember Ted Lasso's catchphrase, "Be a goldfish." According to Jason Sudeikis's lovable character, goldfish have a 10-second memory span (although I did some Google searching and found out it is more like a month). In the blink of an eye, all is forgotten. Just erase that mistake from your memory and move on. You cannot change the past, and you are not defined by one bad performance, but you can improve the future.

Don't Think

Outside of concentrating on the present moment, no other thoughts should creep into your head. If you physically challenge yourself enough, you shouldn't have time to think anyway. *Nothing else matters but the task at hand.* There is nothing to do but compete—all else can wait until after the buzzer goes off. Even the quickest flash of a negative thought will break your flow. And you won't be able to achieve it again. You see it on the tennis court all the time. Someone may have a great headspace going into a game, but then you see them crack under the pressure. They lose a point here and there, then they lose a set. They can't get back their mojo and they end up losing the match. I know that if I go into an event and my thoughts take over, that's when I make mistakes. And I don't like to mess up.

This skill came in handy during the CrossFit Games in 2020, when the Covid pandemic was at its peak. The CrossFit Games were thrown into a tizzy, but, fortunately, they worked out a plan for them to go on. The qualifying stage was done remotely, since most in-person events were canceled. We then had stage 1 Games online before progressing to the final Games, in which the top five (men and women) progressed to an in-person competition on a private ranch in Aromas, California. I continued to train throughout the year—even when others figured there was no point in training because they didn't think that there was going to be a competition. I stayed the course, although I am not going to lie: It was the toughest season yet because I pushed so damn hard while all the work might have been for nothing. The Games might have been canceled at any minute, yet I kept on rowing, just in case. The Games did go on, but there were very strict protocols in place about allowing coaches on the floor only so often. Shane wouldn't even be able to help warm me up as he usually did—right by my side. I felt a pang of sadness as I didn't have him there to share his thoughts on the workouts, especially at this critical final stage. But he had prepared me so well that I knew exactly what I needed to do without even talking to him, and it allowed me to get through the events with confidence and determination. This was a perfect opportunity to let doubts creep in, but since I was so prepared and I trusted in the process, they didn't have a chance. It was so freeing, and I was so proud because I just did the job that I came to do.

Know That It Takes Time

This skill—and it is a skill if you want it to show up consistently—takes years to hone, but, believe me, it is worth it because it is what separates the competitors from the winners. Think of the old story of the turtle and the rabbit—the rabbit was fast, but in the end, the turtle was the winner. It takes time, but once you get it, the high you get off it keeps you going, and you will manage to do things you could only dream of doing before. With any experience, the more you do it, the more you will benefit from it.

The key is to remind yourself of this goal every day. I have stated this before, but it bears repeating: When I am not competing, I still train to compete. I remind myself of my goals at least 20 times a day. I have written them in my notes on my phone and saved it as a screensaver. I have scribbled notes on Post-its around the house. I also write on my bathroom mirror. Examples of my recent training goals:

Hit a 220-pound snatch

Perform an overhead squat with 280 pounds

Perform 75 pull-ups, unbroken 😏

Hold a handstand for longer than 90 seconds

Run sub-5:15 mile and perform 440-pound dead lifts in the same week

WIN THE GAMES!

I don't just read these goals, I say them aloud and I say them boldly. Repetition is important. It's like riding a bike; I do it so many times that one day I don't even think about it, I just do it. That's how I achieve my goals—I say them so often and with so much conviction that they actually come to fruition.

Don't Use It Up

Like a battery, you can deplete your energy source; staying in the zone takes a lot of energy. So only use it when you need it. You will need to recharge, since it doesn't last forever. Find it and use it sparingly. Just like anything in life, too much of a good thing can turn into a bad thing. Throughout my journey, I have been very conscious of not burning out. I have definitely pushed the barriers throughout my career: training for both the CrossFit Games and the Summer Olympics back in 2016; training for both the CrossFit Open and the Commonwealth Games in 2018; and training for the Winter Olympics and the Rogue Invitational in the 2021–2022 CrossFit season. However, with Shane's help, I have been able to understand and set my priorities throughout these experiences and found fulfillment in the process of training for them all and not burning out by switching off when the time is right to recharge and reset. The more you use it, the easier it will be to turn on and off. You'll become more energy-efficient as you'll know when to flip the switch and conserve or when to turn up the heat full-blast.

Find Your Inspo—Wherever You Can

Many performers and athletes listen to music before they are about to pounce on their competitor. It's known, for instance, that Serena Williams hit the court with her headphones and Michael Phelps got psyched up for a race listening to Eminem. I get it—whatever gets you fired up, do it! I don't listen to music in a warm-up because I am minimalistic when it comes to pregaming. Simple and quiet work better for me; besides, I don't want to be dependent on anything. But the stereo blasts at our gym—I love listening to music when I am training, and AC/DC by my Australian brothers-in-arms is my go-to for getting me pumped up. "TNT," "Stiff Up a Lip," "Thunderstruck"—they never get old. I know when Shane wants to see something special in training, he puts on "Back in Black."

Some people get caught up in doing pregaming rituals because they believe they need those to compete at a high level. One competitor may wear "lucky" socks or another may bless themselves right before the buzzer goes off. I try not to have too many rituals because I find they can sap my energy to do my best. Why worry about what socks you're wearing or worry that you didn't listen to the right song to pump you up? Save that energy for the actual event.

READ UP ON WORKING HARD

I read every morning while having my coffee, before I start the day. Sometimes it's for fun, to get me out of my head, but I also read a lot of books by coaches or sports psychologists, even entrepreneurs, to help up my mental game and personal development. The relationship between the mind and the body is incredible, and I love learning more about that connection. I consider it an essential part of training, just like my conditioning pieces, because learning about how my mind works informs me about how I can use it to my best advantage: how to best focus, how to keep out negative thoughts, and how to accept the pain. It's not that the material I read is all that revelatory, but sometimes it can just put a name to something I already instinctively know, sharpen it, and help me strengthen it. For instance, in *Atomic Habits*, James Clear talks about how we human beings really respond to routine. And I found this so fascinating because I've trained my whole life, ever since I was a young girl. From a very young age, I physically trained every single morning, getting up way too early, and late afternoon, after school, to do the work that I needed to do. And now, it's just part of who I am, and it's that discipline that helped train my mind and body to accomplish whatever I've set out to achieve. While I don't enjoy training, I do like pushing myself, and it was cool to see that this kind of discipline was backed up by some science.

Carol Dweck's book *Mindset* was another great book that talked about the mind-body connection. In it, she shows how our lives can be dramatically influenced by how we *think* about our talents and abilities. Those who have a fixed mindset are less likely to thrive than those who believe that talent can be nurtured and developed (the *growth* mindset). I am a firm believer that you need this type of mindset, along with your practice. You can do all the work, but if you don't have the right mindset, then I say it's time to hang up your swim goggles, cleats, or boxing gloves because there isn't any point in moving forward. I know journaling can help a lot with letting the mind reset and feel good. I don't do this as often as I would like, but if my mind is racing, journaling is the best way for me to gather my thoughts and stop myself from overthinking. Writing it all out helps me understand the reason behind my emotions and thoughts.

Focus on Breathing

Letting go of your thoughts is easier said than done. Often, when you're nervous about performing, your breath can become more shallow: You may not take in as much air (and its oxygen) as you should. According to a 2013 article published by the National Library of Medicine, the depletion of oxygen to the brain will cause your focus to plunge, exacerbating your nervousness. The trick is to take four deep breaths—count to four as you inhale deeply through the nose, into the abdomen, and exhale through the mouth, also for four counts. Do this four to five times; this calms your nerves and brings on a sense of calm. I also will do this if I am finding it hard to keep the mind from wandering. Try this the next time you face an overwhelming situation.

Mindfulness and Meditation

While I don't strictly follow a particular religion, I am a spiritual being, and I believe there's a higher power or some universal force that looks out for us. Call it karma, but when you put good energy into the universe, I believe you receive that back. If you feel terrible and don't do anything about it, you're not going to flourish. When I feel off, I find that some sort of meditation is very valuable in helping me get out of my head, and it can help a lot with focus. Even breathing—a simple form of meditation—helps. I am not going to get into some of my hippie ways here, but there is a lot to be said about calming the body down and giving you some headspace.

Meditation doesn't have to be anything formal. Just find a place to sit peacefully so you can let your thoughts leave your head. I think reading and stretching are even forms of meditation—anything that gets your mind to stop racing. Use your breath, adopt a simple mantra, and settle in to quiet your mind. Train your mind to let go of your thoughts so you can quiet them when it is important—on the competition floor.

I believe meditation—or just giving time to yourself to reflect—will stave off any stagnation. To be honest, I know I need to work on this one a bit, as I live a very hectic life, probably committing myself to too many things. I'm also a very high-strung person, and as I mentioned before, I trained vulnerability out of me. I find that meditation can help soften that edge because it allows me to take that time to check in and understand what it is I want to do, where I want to be next, and set goals and expectations for myself. I like stretching as a form of meditation—I can focus on my breathing and clear my mind, slow down, and actually work on my recovery at the same time. For me, it's a win-win situation.

DAILY STRETCHING ROUTINE

I am a big believer in stretching/mobilizing every morning before my day begins. Stretching is not only great for my body, but it allows me to relax and take a moment to get ready for the day ahead. Sometimes if I haven't had enough sleep, I wake up with a little stiffness and soreness from the previous day of training. So while I am stretching and taking 15–20 minutes for myself, I'm waking my body up and preparing it for a full day of training. This also gets my mind in the right frame of mind to start the day off motivated and ready to *work*.

There are two types of stretching: Dynamic stretching—with active movement and repetition—before a session helps to warm the joints, reduce impact injuries, and improve exercise technique. And static stretching—holding a position for 15–30 seconds—after or between sessions will help reduce DOMS (delayed onset muscle soreness) and joint pain. I am also a fan of foam rolling—this will help remove toxins (like lactic acid and carbon dioxide) after exercise and is especially useful for endurance athletes. Personally, I find foam rolling helpful for waking up my legs. If you can afford it, get a massage every so often. Massage is expensive but for good reason: An experienced and knowledgeable sports massage therapist can reduce soreness and tightness and fix all the funk that you accumulate over a long training career. (I get treatment every two weeks during the off-season and once a week during the competitive season.)

Recovery isn't going to make you a world-class athlete overnight or fix a bad approach to training. However, it is a tool at your disposal to become the best athlete you can be and keep coming back at your best. Adding even a few of these methods should make a real difference in the way you feel and perform.

These are a handful of total body stretches I do every morning before training—as well as on my rest days—to keep my body loose, limber, and injury-free. They also help get the blood flowing and the day going. For even more detail, you can find these on my YouTube channel.

LOWER BODY

Seated straddle. On a mat, begin in a seated position with legs stretched out and open to the sides as far as possible. Place your hands on the floor in front of you and walk them forward, resting your forearms on the floor. You can widen your legs if you feel comfortable, breathe, and hold the stretch for 2–3 minutes. If my lower back is winding up a lot, this helps ease that pressure.

Single-leg forward stretch. This is really good for the hamstrings: If they are tight, that will affect the glutes which, in turn, affect the lower back. So if you feel any tightness in these areas, this one is a good go-to. From the position of the seated straddle, bring your right leg in, and stretch your torso forward over the straight left leg. Hold for 2–3 minutes on each side. Breathe into them and never force these stretches—go at your own pace and depth.

Ankle/leg stretch. On a yoga mat, start by sitting on your knees. Come into a lunge on the right foot with your left knee and ankle resting on the mat, then bring the right knee forward past the toes. Hold this position for 30 seconds to 2 minutes (depending on how much time you have) on one leg and then shift to the other leg. You'll feel a stretch through your groin and ankle, but focus on keeping that right heel down on the ground. If you want a little more intensity, you can bring your torso down onto your quad and push your knee closer to the mat. If you have a side that is tighter than the other, spend a bit more time on that tighter side, but always, always, always stretch both sides. If you prioritize one side and neglect the other, it can lead to injury.

Hip stretch. Starting in a lunge position, bring your front knee up so that it's directly over the ankle, and place the other knee farther back. Sit a bit more upright. Let your right hip sink to the mat as much as you can to feel that pulling sensation through the hip and the groin area. This is great for really tight hip flexors. When I do this, I can also feel it in through my hamstrings. If you hold this pose for a bit longer, you can push the knee out (careful, not too much) for an inner-thigh stretch. You can also come down onto your elbows if you want to feel more of a stretch—it depends on your flexibility. Make sure that knee doesn't extend over your toe, as in the previous stretch. You also want to stretch into that chest and pec area—opening that chest up is so important, particularly for those who have more of a desk job. We can get really tight in our chest and tend to curl over our computers; then our posture goes out the window. Our shoulders get rotated and tight, and this is the perfect stretch to really loosen up that chest area and allow you to regain that posture. Again, make sure you do this on both sides, holding each for a minute or two.

UPPER BODY

Shoulder stretch. Lying down on your stomach, legs out, stretch the left arm out to the side. With your right palm underneath your right shoulder, push into the floor to roll over to the left side of the body. If you feel up to it, you can bend your right leg and place it on the mat behind you for a slight spinal twist. You can play with how intense you want to be—carefully. You don't want to overdo it. This feels great in the shoulders and upper back. Hold for 30 seconds to a minute, and don't forget the other side!

The puppy dog. Kneeling, place your hands out on the mat in front and bring your chest down as low to the mat as possible. Stick your butt in the air and press your chest into the ground. You should feel that sensation all through your lat area, which really helps that chest open up. If you want to make this stretch more intense, you can grab a block and put your hands on top so that your chest can drop further down. Tight lats can lead to a lot of upper back and trap problems, so making sure that you're nice and loose in the upper body is super important.

Frog's pose. I could sit in this pose all day. Sitting on your knees with your buttocks on your ankles, lean forward with your arm outstretched to feel the pull in your lats. Pushing your chest toward the floor as much as you can (without pain) can apply additional pull to the lats for a deeper stretch.

I can't reiterate enough how important it is when you're stretching not to force anything because you never want to put your body through too much strain. Just slowly breathe through the stretches and slowly get deeper into them only when it feels good. It is also key not to rush through them and to hold these from about 30 seconds to 2 minutes.

Taper: Deep in the Trenches

Much like getting ready for a marathon, where runners will taper their running a week before the race, I taper my training in the days leading up to the CrossFit Games or any other big event where I'm competing. As I train, I push my body to the edge for months—Shane calls it "deep in the trenches"—so I need to rest before the big competition. This is where I dial everything back or, as Shane likes to say, "sharpen the sword." It gives me a breather to recharge that battery so I am revved up for competition.

Shane likes to think mechanically when training athletes, and he compares the forging of a sword to the way we train. The first step in sword making is gathering the materials and tools. This means making a plan and having our PRVN team around us. The next step starts with thrusting that shapeless block of steel into the fire. This would be our first phase of training, starting out with three hours a day. Then once we've heated the steel and it's ready for molding, we start hammering it, flattening it, reheating it, and sanding it, which is like molding the athlete in the peak conditioning phases. Now we are up to 6–8 hours a day. Once we are in top form, we next need to prepare for competition; these last steps are what we call sharpening the sword. Much like the last phase of forging a sword, this is a series of heating and sharpening. We work 12–13 hours a day to hone and polish and finally taper. In the end, this lengthy process has created a beautifully smooth but sharp object, primed for action.

Have a Lifeline

Because I train so intensely for months, I tend to get so drained that I break emotionally in the lead-up to a big competition. My mind starts to wander and I start to ask questions that aren't good for me and doubt everything: *Am I doing enough? Did I put in my absolute all? Can I pull out another win this year?* I ask such self-sabotaging questions even though I know I can reign another year. This is when I fall back on my team for reassurance, particularly Shane and my dad. They won't offer blind sympathy, but instead they ask me the questions that I will have to answer with confidence.

In 2017, when all I wanted was to win the CrossFit Games, it had been just a few weeks out before Shane and I were heading to America, and I needed one of my calls with Dad. I was getting worked up and allowing my thoughts to be clouded by how depleted I felt. I needed a bit of reassurance from someone who was going to give it to me straight. I didn't need to be judged nor did I want sympathy. He reminded me of where I was in my training.

"Sure, you are tired and sore—you are right now in the trenches. Of course, you don't feel like you can win. You have zero energy and what energy you do have, you are devoting to training." His words helped recenter my thoughts, and they especially simplified things for me and helped lift that sense of feeling overwhelmed. I could get back to focusing on the prize.

What started out as an SOS to my dad has now become regular practice. This pep talk was something I wouldn't quite understand in my earlier years as an athlete, but I now understand that it's my way of confirming that I am doing enough to win and not getting complacent in my success. And because it helps me solidify my readiness, my calls to Dad have become a regular part of my preparation leading up to the games. Some of my favorite Dad quotes:

"Remember, it's not the size of the dog in the fight but the size of the fight in the dog," my dad would tell me, adding to just forget about winning.

"You can't control that. Don't worry about the things you can't control. No one knows what the programming is going to look like. Just do your absolutely best right now, and I guarantee you will level up to whatever they throw at you on the day. I am proud of you not because of your results but that you are working so damn hard."

"Tia, the leaderboard is back at zero [after every competition/event], so give it everything and know those women are going to be fighting just as hard as you."

"I want to see how big your heart is, Tia. Everyone out there is fit and can do this, but it's about who has the biggest heart. Who wants it more? Go out there and show me how strong your heart is, because I know what you're capable of."

My favorite of them all: "When you put your head on the pillow at night, ask yourself: Did I give it my absolute best today?" If I can answer yes, then I know I am in a good place. There are a few times I have called to tell him, "Dad, I didn't give it my best. I can do better. But I just didn't have it in me that day. . . ." And he'd respond, "That's okay. Because you know what? Tomorrow you're going be even better and you will make up for your efforts today."

Everyone has doubts—it's good to work through them, and even better if you have someone you can lean on while you're doing so. That way, for me, I leave any doubt behind so I have none during competition—I can just go out and get into the zone.

Visualization

The more I compete, the more I can get into this focused state as it gets easier and easier to summon without as much effort. And the more I entered these flow states, I started to see myself differently. I started visualizing and looking at myself as a champion, and that is the difference between the Tia who was just starting out and not realizing her true potential and the Tia today who has stood at the top of the podium multiple times straight, becoming the most dominant CrossFit athlete of all time.

More specifically, visualization can help in the lead-up to an important game or competition. I visualize going through every movement, every detail. I see myself out on the floor, stepping up onto that platform, waiting for Boz (the head judge) to give me the GO signal, and calmly but with a lot of adrenaline beginning to set up in my clean position. I then see myself first finding the bar directly over my shoelaces, then placing my right hand on the bar, just outside of my leg, followed by the left hand. I then begin to move my bum up to activate my hamstrings and set my legs in a low squat, acting as springs, ready to be released. When I feel ready, I begin to initiate the pull by driving my legs into the ground and the bar is being pulled up as I reach full extension, before floating in the air momentarily until I begin to move my body down under the barbell, ready to receive it as gravity begins to let it drop onto me. I absorb the weight in the front of my shoulders and collarbones and then gradually ride the weight down before driving the legs through the ground again to stand the weight back up.

With such vivid replay, I train my brain so it is not a totally new sensation when I actually do the event. And by now I have performed a clean so many times that my muscle memory knows what to do. At the risk of sounding like a broken record, that's why training and doing the repetitions are crucial to your success. You are marrying the body and mind, getting them to connect on a subconscious level, which allows you to take your abilities to a new level.

There is an important distinction to be made between visualizing yourself as a champion while you train and competing. I never want to visualize winning while competing because that places too much stress on the outcome. If you overemphasize that, you'll start putting too much pressure on yourself. Stay in the present, not the future or the past; slow everything down and do what you need to do to execute and anticipate anything that could happen—but don't visualize the actual moment of winning. Game day is all about execution. Winning is merely the by-product.

Smile

I will leave you with this parting tip to keep in the flow: Smile—not for other people but for yourself. It lifts your spirits, helps release cortisol and endorphins, and increases your endurance. It's important to remember to enjoy the journey and find happiness in everything you do—even through the pain.

CHAPTER 10

Give It a Rest

Recovery Is Key for the Body and the Mind

With all the time I have spent in America, I have noticed another big difference between Aussies and Americans. Americans live to work; Australians work to live. This holds true in all aspects of life, and I see it at full tilt at many CrossFit gyms across the United States. Some people get so caught up in trying to achieve a goal that they've forgotten to enjoy the process (I'm talking from experience here, and you now know how I love the process). More importantly, they also forget to take time *off* from the process. I get it—I can get caught up in all the "Go, go, go!" mentality, too. But I know that it can only end in disaster. In my career, I have observed many people who strive to reach their goal, putting so much pressure on themselves, both inside and outside the gym. And that can be detrimental to their state of mind as well as how they perform as an athlete.

Don't be mistaken: There is nothing wrong with being ambitious, but you can't spread yourself too thin, and you need to ensure that you are giving yourself the necessary rest to recharge. I now know—from a lot of experience—that rest and recovery are where all the magic happens.

The Mind Needs to Recover

I've always been a big believer in having a balance between all-out training sessions and allowing some downtime to rest. I know that rest is needed to help promote both a physiological recovery and a mental reboot. Shane and I make sure that break is a total respite from our workday life, just like other normal couples. We take off our coach-athlete hats, as well as our business owner hats (when we can), and just are Shane and Tia, husband and wife. We leave work behind for most evenings, even though it can be tough to do so, especially leading up to an important competition. There is a time and a place to talk shop and that is not when we are on the couch watching a movie and trying to relax. You won't hear me talk about what's coming up tomorrow in training. Occasionally, I do find myself wanting to talk about the day's training, but I have to stop myself and remember that it's not the time to worry about that.

Besides taking evenings off, I always have one rest day a week and that is typically a Monday. This day is intentional: We are roughly mimicking the week of the CrossFit Games, which typically start on a Tuesday or Wednesday and go throughout the weekend. Smaller competitions typically run from Friday to Sunday. When Sunday night comes around, Shane and I, after working so hard all week, go out and treat ourselves to the movies (my go-to candy is M&Ms; his are soft lollies—it's an Australian candy) or we go out to dinner at a nice restaurant. That time off can be so rewarding—it makes us look forward to something at the end of the week while we are working hard. It's also a night when we have guilt-free cheat meals; we sometimes overindulge, but we know we've earned it as we've eaten clean and healthy all week long.

I need this weekly ritual of relaxation to look forward to; otherwise the training starts to feel overwhelming. I may feel overloaded and start thinking, *Oh, man, this is so boring and I have so many more months to go.* But giving yourself a break, a moment away from all that intensity, does wonders for your sense of well-being. Time away from such intense pressure offers you an objectivity that you may not have if you are constantly under stress. It gives you a breather to put everything aside and not think about it. These moments off from training replenish my energy stores as well, emotionally and mentally. So, remember to counteract the intensity of your workouts with a break that will give you a sense of recovery and rejuvenation. You will find yourself heading back to the gym feeling fresh and with a renewed sense of motivation.

My competitive career has a short shelf life, and I have a very small window to capitalize on my brand and build a legacy in time for my retirement from competition. So, it can be very easy for me to become impatient. It's hard not to feel the clock ticking and give in to the pressure of having to do everything at once. I therefore will try to pile everything up, thinking, *I need to do more, more, more.* We have learned the hard way, though, that we need to manage how much we take on, so we implemented twice-yearly check-ins to make sure we are not falling into our individual and collective traps of trying to do everything ourselves. For me, I knew it was necessary to take a full season off from training and competing after the 2022 Games, not just because of my back or because I hadn't had an off-season in over two years, never mind that I was pregnant! Wouldn't you know it, though, I found myself almost committing to two events that would have required me to train and compete throughout the off-season (I don't like opportunities sliding past me). If it weren't for the people close to me who reeled me in from overextending myself, I would have taken them on and drained myself physically, mentally, and emotionally.

The Body Needs Time to Recover . . .

Many in competitive sports feel bad about taking a day off—it reminds me of the corporate mentality of an ambitious go-getter feeling the need to be the first one in and the last one out of the office. The number of hours in the gym feels like its own competition. This isn't good for your body. You'll just injure yourself or reinjure yourself. I have to remind myself of this every day, especially during the lead-up to a big competition.

Also, if you don't give yourself time to recover, come game time you can jeopardize your power in your performance and, in the long run, increase your chances of just burning out. My dad always has a way of helping me stay aware of this trap, and he asks (often), "Tia, you aren't burning the candle at both ends, are you?" I can't help but think sometimes, *Yes, I am!* but his reminder gives me the chance to check myself and make sure that it's not getting out of hand and hindering my training (which will, in turn, hinder my performance—which defeats the purpose, am I right?!). Because if you want something so much that you work at it nonstop, you put yourself in a position to feel burned out and defeated, which will only be completely counterproductive to your goals.

It has long been proven that rest promotes muscle recovery and aids repair throughout the body. Studies show that taking at least 24 hours helps the body replenish your energy stores and repairs damaged tissues from pushing your body to extremes. Plain and simple, rest is just as important as your workout, and not only for the body but for the mind as well. Resting is not a selfish thing; it is absolutely necessary. Again, I reference a great question my dad always asks me: "Tia, who is the most important person in your life?"

"Well, Shane, you, Mum, my sisters, and Willow," I always respond.

"No, *you* are the most important person on this planet. You know why? Because, if you don't prioritize yourself and ensure that your health and well-being are in good shape, how can you help and show your love to those people you care about? I need to make sure I am mentally and physically healthy to provide my best for you, your mother, and your sisters—that is how I can be the best husband and father."

So true. I can't be of any help to Shane, Willow, and my other loved ones if I am not healthy myself—physical, mentally, and emotionally. That is more important than any competition or job position in life.

A TYPICAL DAY OF TRAINING: WAKE UP, GRIND, EXECUTE, REPEAT

I train 10 hours a day, especially during the period leading up to the Cross-Fit Games.

6:00 a.m.: Up and at 'em. Coffee, stretch, then to a 75-minute swimming workout.

8:00 a.m.: Breakfast made by Shane (Husband of the Year). I eat throughout the day, but he's very conscious of making sure I eat right and consume enough calories to keep up with my exertion.

10:00 a.m.: I hit the track for some running intervals and some sprinting drills.

Noon: Head to the gym, eat lunch there, mobilize (stretch) and rest for a little bit before we get into our gym session.

1–6 p.m.: The gym session consists of 7–9 pieces: warm-up, 2–3 barbell strength/skill pieces, a barbell/conditioning piece, a gymnastic straight/ skill piece, 1–2 conditioning pieces, accessories (movements that supplement the main conditioning exercises), and possibly a long aerobic conditioning piece. I will often hop in the sauna and/or an ice bath to promote muscle recovery.

7 p.m.: Dinner and watch TV. We try to keep up with all the great streaming shows. It is tough to do during training season!

8 p.m.: My time to hit the emails and attend to computer work that I didn't get to throughout the day.

9 p.m.: Bedtime. I aim for a minimum of 8 hours of zzz's a day, but I like to get 10, if possible (read: if Willow lets me). I notice if I don't get 10-plus hours of sleep a night, my body doesn't recover as well.

. . . But Not Too Much Time

Don't get me started on weekend warriors. Those people who only go to the gym on odd Saturdays every other month. They are inevitably stuck in a loop of constant soreness. They will work out one day like a fiend, which will make them sore, but then not return until days later. They recover, but since they don't come back in until the next weekend, their bodies work at a deficit; they are always running behind the curve and making it much harder for themselves to progress. If they committed to two or three more days, they would find that they're actually building up that important muscle memory and stamina. It's like they are starting from scratch. Every. Single. Time.

Note: If you are reading this and are thinking, *Oh boy, this is me*, I highly recommend that you get into a habit of doing something active at a minimum of four to five times a week. I am sure you have a very busy life, but figure out what works for you. If you are committed to a healthy lifestyle, you will find a better way to fit it in. I can sympathize, as I even have to work at this: In my off-season, I am often swamped by so much computer work or so many travel commitments with sponsors or appearances that I struggle to find time. I figured out that I need to exercise in the mornings; otherwise, the day slips by. Before you know it, it is 7 p.m. and, just like many of you, I simply don't feel like doing anything because my mind is so drained from the day's work of calls, emails, and meetings. But I know that committing to regular exercise can stimulate the brain and give me a new sense of energy. Even after a simple 30- to 45-minute exercise session, I inevitably feel refreshed. I'm telling you it's just about building a habit. The jury is out on whether working out in the morning or evening is better; what is certain is doing it in the first place and sticking to it will get you where you want to be.

To figure out that balance, you need to understand what your priorities are. To people on the outside, for instance, it may look like I don't have a balance in my life, especially when

I am close to an important competition. They see me at the gym for hours on end and, more likely than not, I am skipping Monday rest days. But I've prioritized my goals in a way that is very manageable. It is the decision I made—and there is a time limit. I know my priorities, and my priorities at the CrossFit Games are to win. When the Games are over (and I won), I tip the scales back to the other side a bit to have more relaxation and turn down the training—because I deserve it and my team needs it. I realize that this won't be forever—we are mortal souls after all. Shane and I long ago signed up for the scales being a bit skewed every time we go into competition—knowing that after my shelf life, we want to have a family. When it is close to Games time, the scales are skewed heavily to the side of training, and only training. Some people may see me and think I work too hard and push too much, but I know what I need to do for now, with the understanding that this way of life isn't forever. If that means I miss out on a huge party or a wedding because I'm two weeks out from a major competition, so be it. It would have been a lot of fun, of course, but it would be a distraction and possibly lead to a setback in my performance. There is a dance between being open-minded and taking opportunities as they come, but you also need to be focused and dialed in to where your priorities lie. The right people in your life will understand and get on board; if they don't, well, maybe they aren't the right people in your life.

Active Recovery

There is one day—usually in the middle of the week—when I take what I call an "active recovery" day. Active recovery sessions are low-impact and low-volume exercises aimed to accelerate the body's recovery responses, but it's also a great way to mix up your training and break the tedium of training in the same environment. I like to drop the weights and get outdoors by walking, hiking, or swimming. It's a low-intensity day, when I focus on the heart rate more than anything. We'll focus on what is called zone 2 training or low-HR (heart-rate) training, which is great for endurance and recovery. (There are a total of six heart-rate zones with zone 1 being the lowest intensity [i.e., watching TV on the couch], and zone 6 as the highest [running the fastest sprint possible].) Zone 2 is something like a light jog without getting out of breath—your heart rate should max out somewhere between 60 percent and 70 percent. We use this as a training tool, as it is a really great form of endurance training. I don't race the clock or strain the body—it's all about keeping the blood flowing while destressing the mind. Usually it entails another sport—swimming, bike riding, running—for about 60 to 90 minutes. I give the body a reason to move, but not at an aggressive pace. I favor swimming on these days: Being immersed in water offers a much-needed break for my joints, and I feel my body recovering just by its buoyancy. And, remember: Swimming is a great sport for expanding the lung capacity (as my dad constantly reminds me).

Mix It Up

Working professionals and athletes alike can often get so consumed in their chosen field that they burn themselves out. I don't want you to burn out. To keep you from doing that, you need to mix it up. This is exactly the reason I took on bobsled. A lot of CrossFitters would have turned that opportunity down out of a concern that it would affect their training regimen. But I saw the experience as a way to give me three wins: (1) It created so many other opportunities even if many thought it would jeopardize my CrossFit season; (2) it offered me the kind of break from CrossFit that gave me an even better appreciation for the sport; and (3) it provided an avenue to help keep me stimulated.

Mixing it up doesn't have to be taken to an extreme, such as trying out for the Olympics; you could just do a day of swimming or skiing. Sometimes Shane and I take the PRVN Fitness team rock climbing or out to play beach volleyball to change up the training and help activate different muscles—and, of course, this kind of venture adds a little spark of fun.

Listen to Your Body

All of this is to say listen to your body. If you are tired, rest. If you need a break, take a break, even if that means changing it up and doing another activity or sport. Your body knows best. And when it is injured, it will tell you. I should have listened to my back in 2014, but I let the injury fester, and it set me back 12 months of competition.

It is all about being attuned to your body—is it a slight muscle strain or does it feel worse than that? You, of course, want to have a level of soreness—that means something is changing, getting stronger, developing for the better. But nothing should be so painful that you can barely walk or get out of bed. Put your ego aside, and let it rest. One rest day is better than two weeks off or, worse, missing an important competition down the road. Being pregnant only emphasized for me how much the body tells you. When I was pregnant, I would wake up every day and check in with it. Was I good to go to the gym? If I felt tired, I sometimes opted for a long walk instead.

As for smaller injuries, what I call "niggles," be sure to give them TLC before they turn into something bigger. Maybe your chest or quads are too tight because you haven't spent the right amount of time loosening them up after training and they give you a referred pain in your shoulder or knee. I always try to find a great sports massage therapist who can take care of all these niggles, and I will tailor my training in a way that still has me listening to my body. So, if something hurts, but I'm still able to do the movement, I'll train through it. I know the difference between a small niggle that can be a simple fix with sports massage or some stretching, compared to something more serious. Before and after, I'll give it a bit of love. If it's an injury that doesn't appear to be getting better that's in the lower body—say, my ankle or knee—I'll skip a lower-body workout for that day or two, and I'll concentrate on the upper body. If I have a sore shoulder, I'll do a lot of squatting and a lot of lower-body movements. Again, it all comes back to being attuned to your body.

My Go-Tos for Recovery

Fire and Ice

Heat and cold—our bodies like a bit of stress, but not too much. When we use extreme heat or extreme cold, our bodies react to that stress by cleaning up, repairing and restoring our cells, and taming any inflammation. How to know which is better for you? I change it up, depending on how my body feels or whatever it responds better to in the moment.

For extreme cold, I often do ice baths, the practice of taking a 10- to 15-minute dip in very cold water (45°F–50°F), and when I really need relief, I'll even take a full-on ice bath after an intense workout. While there are some conflicting studies about the effectiveness of cold therapy, a lot of informal research has shown there are real health benefits: It boosts your metabolism, combats inflammation, promotes lymphatic drainage, and improves blood circulation. It also has been shown to alleviate muscle soreness. The cold, especially, helps ease the intensity of tenderness that kicks in 24 to 48 hours after exercise, or delayed onset muscle soreness (DOMS). So it's perfect after a long day of competition to feel good for the next day. I began this throughout competition back in 2015 and have never looked back. I started out slowly and played around with timing—between three minutes one week and four minutes the next; that allows the DOMS not to be as severe the next day. Throughout competition, I will sit in the ice bath every so often—it depends on how bad the day was. If, for example, it is a really hot day, I will sit in the ice bath to cool myself down. I wouldn't say I *love* taking ice baths—but I know it is great for my muscle soreness. I think it comes down to the person, again listening to the body and seeing if you notice improvements to recovery.

For heat, I recommend sauna therapy, which has been around for thousands of years. Sitting in the sauna at 175°F–200°F heat will increase your body temperature, boost blood flow, pump up the heart rate, and lower your blood pressure. It has also been shown to stimulate muscle growth, improve cognition, and strengthen the immune system. Again, this type of healthy stress on the body can heal and repair itself. The heat also helps flush out toxins as you sweat and cool the body down, so I like to hydrate throughout this process. The blood and the oxygen in your body help repair muscle damage. Because you're warm, you're generating that heat needed for your muscles to do repair work. You don't have to physically do anything, yet you are actively helping your body recover by allowing your joints, tendons, ligaments, and muscles to heal without putting them under any strain.

I noticed how well the heat worked for me during 2020. Because of the Covid shutdown, I wasn't regularly jumping in the sauna after training, and I was having a lot more aches and pains throughout my body—more than normal. So Shane and I bought our own sauna (list that under what the pandemic makes you do!), and as soon as I put it back into my regular routine, I felt better. From then on, it has been a regular practice. Depending on the time of year and what I have physically done during that day, I will determine how much time I need to spend in the sauna. But, as a rule, during the winter months, I'm in there for at least 20 minutes. During summer, I do less since I typically will have already sweated a lot: about 10–15 minutes. I'll do this a minimum of three times a week.

I also found it beneficial to contrast both heat and cold in training, so I'll spend three minutes in the sauna then three minutes in the ice bath, then two minutes in the sauna, two minutes in the ice, one minute in the sauna, one minute in ice. I'll do this a minimum of three times a week. *Note*: Heat therapy and ice therapy are not for everyone. Please check with your doctor before trying any sort of therapy, especially if you have preexisting cardiovascular disease or high blood pressure. This is not for the faint of heart (and maybe not for some with heart problems).

Nutrition

Seriously, you are what you eat. Good nutrition is crucial for everyone's overall health and even more so for athletes. There is no doubt about it: You will feel it if you don't eat right. And you need to eat enough, not just because it will make you feel good but because it will give you energy. Before I came across Cross-Fit and started to learn about nutrition, I would have chocolate in the morning and forget to eat throughout the day until dinner because I was so busy (so I thought). Sorry, Mum—I grew up on really healthy food, but when I left home, I just didn't keep it up. To be honest, I just didn't think too much about it. But once I started to learn about good nutrition and started consuming a healthier diet, my body felt so much better. I ate cleaner, upped my daily calorie intake, and made sure I ate a consistent amount of protein, carbohydrates, and fats (I love fats). I became a completely different person—more energized, happier, and definitely healthier.

Macronutrient and Micronutrient Ratios

I have dabbled in a variety of trendy diets throughout the years, starting with the paleo diet (didn't everyone?) when I first got into CrossFit, then experimenting with vegan and vegetarianism. I learned about fasting, too, but none have really worked for me. I was either eating too much or too little so I decided to keep it simple and follow a macro approach. This is all about macronutrients—carbohydrates, proteins, and fats—the main nutrients that help our bodies function properly. Finding the right balance among these three is key to how we maximize our health, for sure, but also our levels of performance and recovery. You can tailor your protein, carbohydrate, and fat ratios to suit your own goals. For me, this type of diet ensures that I eat the right portion sizes and types of food for my body to perform at its best. Typically, my macros are: proteins—140g; carbohydrates—235g; and fats—55g. This helps me maintain a consistent body weight of 138 pounds for my CrossFit training and if I need to lose weight for weight lifting, I can easily lose 4 pounds with just a few small changes. While I don't have a specific breakdown of macros for each meal, I do take into account my training schedule.

Like my overall caloric intake, my macronutrient ratios also change throughout the year, based on the competition season and my body's need for additional recovery. During the months of the off-season, I like to give my body a much-needed break from the low-fat, high-carb pounding it has become accustomed to during Games training. By upping my natural and healthy fats and lowering my carbohydrates, I can effectively restore hormone balance, increase nutrient levels, and support overall cell function, which helps me get a refreshed mind, body, and soul as I prepare for the season ahead. As we move through the season, I gradually increase my overall calorie intake as well as my macronutrient ratios. Whereas a typical off-season ratio may look like 40 percent carbs, 30 percent protein, and 30 percent fat, I will move to more of a carb-heavy diet as the season ramps up, progressing to well above 50 percent carbs and under 20 percent fat at my peak, allowing my body to optimally recover. Micronutrients should also be at the forefront of each athlete's nutrition plan, no matter what diet you follow. I make sure I get a healthy dose of some key micronutrients whether it is through whole foods or supplementation, such as vitamin D, B-complex vitamins, calcium, magnesium, and zinc.

TYPICAL TRAINING DAILY DIET

My daily food intake differs from day to day, depending on where I am and how I am feeling throughout training. Since that can be up as high as 2,800 calories on a training day. I am smaller than many CrossFitters and have never been a big eater (sometimes it's a challenge to consume so much!), but it's essential for me to have enough energy for training, day after day. I need the large calorie intake!

Breakfast
Bagel, eggs, turkey bacon, avocado. Side of fruit and yogurt.

Snack
Banana and a muesli bar.

Lunch
Leftovers from previous night's dinner; spaghetti Bolognese, a veggie stir-fry, flavored mince, and rice.

Afternoon Snack
Oatmeal mixed with blueberries, maple syrup, and yogurt.

Dinner
Steak and veggies, lasagna, spaghetti Bolognese, veggie stir-fry, tacos, or a curry. Something that I enjoy and makes me feel full for the next day of training.

Dessert
Cup of tea, with some biscuits, some chocolate. Something satisfying but nothing too rich.

I keep it simple and give my body the best chance by sticking to whole foods wherever possible to get an adequate amount of protein, carbohydrates, and fat: high-quality cuts of meat, fish, and lots of fruit and veggies. Fresh is best, good-quality protein should be your main go-tos, and stay away from processed foods and sugar. Timing meals correctly will also improve your recovery. Early in my career, I used to eat only a few large meals a day, which led to an overall feeling of

> lethargy and energy fluctuations. Ever since I learned more about meal timing, I have been able to find a good balance about what foods to eat and their caloric intake between sessions, making the most of my recovery time.

Calories In, Calories Out

Total daily energy expenditure (TDEE) is the calculation of calories you burn during the day. For a professional athlete, the most important factor throughout the season is our physical activity level or what we call "training volume." I like to keep food journals or use tracking apps to monitor my daily food intake, while also working with Shane to adjust my intake based on my current volume of training. For example, during the peak months of May, June, and July, my training volume is significantly higher than in the months prior, and sometimes even double or triple the amount of the off-season months. So it was extremely important for us to monitor my food consumption closely, because even one week of undereating during high-volume periods could mean massive mishaps in energy and performance in the gym, and even possible risk of injury due to lack of recovery and poor sleep. For the more general athlete, while tracking physical activity is important, most of these individuals will not fluctuate in their training volume throughout the year. This means that tracking basal metabolic rate (BMR) becomes increasingly vital. BMR represents the caloric needs of our body at rest or while we are sedentary, so even if these athletes cannot commit to working out every day, they will be able to adjust their calories to stay above or below their BMR and activity level threshold, depending on their goals.

My rule of thumb is to stick to easily digestible foods with a high glycemic index (meaning they're faster-absorbing) around my training windows and have more calorically and nutrient-dense foods in the early morning and after training.

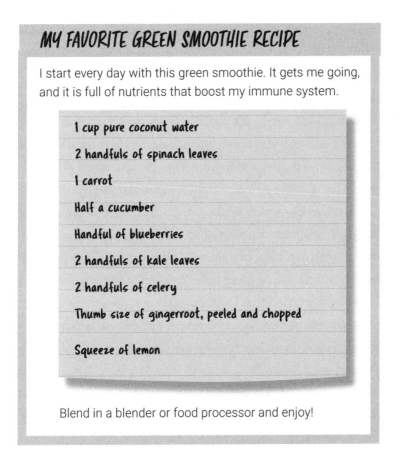

MY FAVORITE GREEN SMOOTHIE RECIPE

I start every day with this green smoothie. It gets me going, and it is full of nutrients that boost my immune system.

1 cup pure coconut water

2 handfuls of spinach leaves

1 carrot

Half a cucumber

Handful of blueberries

2 handfuls of kale leaves

2 handfuls of celery

Thumb size of gingerroot, peeled and chopped

Squeeze of lemon

Blend in a blender or food processor and enjoy!

Depending on where I am in the season and what my training looks like, my daily calorie intake on training days can range from about 2,400 to 2,800 calories. On rest days, the intake is generally around 2,100 to 2,200 calories because I am not exerting as much energy. Sometimes I have to force myself to eat; rest days I hit about the needed calories and I am so full that I struggle to eat more, but I know I need to for my health and for my performance. It's crucial to adjust your nutritional intake to suit your training schedule, especially if you follow a CrossFit plan that is always different from one week to the next. In that case, it's crucial to adjust your water and food consumption to suit your schedule.

My calorie intake has definitely increased over the years. When I was training for weight lifting and was competing in the 128-pound category division, I would consume 1,800 calories a day in order to lose weight and prepare for competition. (It's important to train at the weight you compete in, so your body acclimates over time and you don't feel too depleted during competition.) The one thing I found very challenging leading up to and during competition was this: Because I couldn't eat more, I worried that I was potentially stripping my body of muscle mass, not fat, because I was so lean already. I didn't want to jeopardize my strength while eating so few calories a day, so I did it—very carefully. It is about finding a good balance—we don't want to strip either too much fat or too much muscle because that will mess with your hormones and overall health. Once I moved to the United States and no longer competed in

weight lifting, I was able to forget about body-weight categories and could up my calories. I also noticed an improvement in
my training and performance. I felt stronger, I recovered faster,
and I had so much more energy throughout training. I know
this because not only was my resting heart rate a lower number
in the mornings with the same amount of sleep, but I felt more
focused, and because of that I trained better.

Losing Weight

When I first discovered CrossFit, I was no more than 115
pounds. When I decided to try my hand at weight lifting a few
months later, I needed to put on weight because I was told I
would best perform in the 128-pound category. To do that, I
had to eat heaps of food to weigh more at weigh-in for my
early competitions, but as I started to develop muscle and gain
weight, I deliberately trained at 132 pounds and would lose
4–5 pounds before competition. The 4–5-pound loss would be
done over the course of four to six weeks. We came to this rela-
tively slow time period by a lot of trial and error. If I lost the
weight in a shorter amount of time, I would feel depleted. The
time frame of four to six weeks out from competition allowed
me to go into a competition with the lost weight but also really
strong. As I explained earlier, I needed to slowly lose weight so
my body would adapt better under the load at my new body
weight and to make sure I wasn't losing muscle throughout this
process. When I am not training for weight lifting and just

focusing on CrossFit, I do find it hard to accept being slightly heavier. Shane always encourages me to train for the Games around 140–142 pounds so it's a little easier when it comes to odd objects or rucking and doing workouts in vests.

When I tried out for the bobsled team, I would need to put on more weight. Isn't it funny that, when you finally get comfortable with yourself, something else comes around the corner to shake you up? At the time I was 138 pounds, and I needed to gain 20 pounds. I needed more weight to propel that initial start off the block, which allows us to go down the track faster.

I admit that the weight gain physically affected my performance (not to mention potentially sabotaging my hard-won acceptance of my body). Rather than the power it should have given me, it felt like an anchor; it slowed me down. My body hadn't adequately adjusted to the rapid weight increase. I could tell because my reaction from my brain was still firing, but my body felt a fraction of a second slower than normal. I clearly remembered to factor that in on our timing calls on race days. (A timing call is when, as the brakeman, I shout to let the driver know to get ready for my push. I'd yell, "READY, BACK, SET," and then we would explode off the blocks and hit the ice as hard as we could with every step I took.) It probably had something to do with how fast I had to increase my body weight—I had to gain it in about two months. My body didn't have time to adjust by eating an excessive amount of calories every day. (I averaged 3,800 to 4,300 a day for three months.) Gorging made everything in my body feel slow and tired. I felt as slow as a tortoise. It was also so important for me to eat good foods so the pounds I did put on weren't just fat. The easy thing to do was just eat McDonald's fast food every day and not train as much, but that wasn't going to help me be fast or powerful. What I needed to put on was muscle, not fat. Shane would cook me breakfast every morning: five eggs, five strips of turkey bacon. I would put those eggs and bacon on a bagel to make a sandwich. I would also have a second bagel, cut in half with one half spread with peanut butter, the other half with blackberry jam. (This probably sounds amazing to you, but it took me about 35 minutes to eat it all and by the time bobsled season was over, I didn't want to see this meal ever again!)

When bobsled ended, CrossFit came back on. And I had to turn around and then *lose* the 20 pounds to get back into shape for the '22 Open. As fast as I put it on, I had to lose all of it even faster, as the 2022 CrossFit season began in less than a week. Not only did I need to lose that weight, but I also had to get back into a fitness regimen that I had stopped over the bobsled season. As the pounds melted off, however, I definitely started to feel more like myself. Healthier. Faster. More nimble. Everything started to fall back into place, although I was still smarting from the Olympics outcome. As heartbreaking as it was, though, I know I was not alone in such disappointment—it happens to so many athletes around the world by luck and fate. One silver lining: It did make me appreciate CrossFit even more, because I never have to worry about Australia giving my spot to someone else. It was up to me and only me.

Hydration

More than food, though, water is *everything*. Our bodies are about 60 percent water, so drinking enough is essential for our bodies to function. For casual athletes, there is a general rule of thumb: Drink half an ounce of water per pound of body weight each day at the very minimum. Competitive athletes need to be a little more cognizant of their hydration levels, as many factors can affect hydration and electrolyte levels while training. (I make sure I drink about 72 ounces of water a day.) Also remember: What you sweat out you must put back in, and this includes key electrolytes and vitamins as well. If you feel sick, drink water, if you are tired, drink water, if you are hungry and don't have any food on you, drink water. I try to drink pretty regularly throughout the day so I optimize my training. When it comes time to compete, I add electrolytes to my water to help my body hold the fluids. I never want to be too depleted. Supplements such as salt, citric acid, magnesium, and potassium can all be very beneficial when you're feeling dehydrated, especially when you're competing outside in the summertime or in warmer climates.

I always keep a bottle of water handy: You'd be amazed at how much more water you'll drink just by having it nearby—especially in the winter months.

However, you can drink *too* much. If you drink more than what your kidneys can handle (about a quart of fluid every hour), the excess will be retained in your body, and that can cause a serious condition known as hyponatremia, or "water intoxication." A mild form may cause confusion, nausea, and vomiting, but in more serious cases it can cause swelling in the brain and perhaps be fatal. It is rare, so I don't want to scare you, but it can happen, especially during competitions and intense training, when you are tempted to overhydrate.

To avoid dehydration, Shane likes to perform sweat tests on me. It is a great way to see how much water and sodium I am losing. We do this a couple of ways—one is scientific: Using a strip kit, we measure my pH level. You want it to be slightly acidic, not too much and not too alkaline. We also do it the nonscientific way: We keep a record of how many times I use the toilet. If I go a lot, I am nicely hydrated. If I am not going a lot, I am not well hydrated. Again, listen to your body—it will tell you what you need.

While we are on the topic of hydration, let's talk about two possible sabotours, caffeine and alcohol. I am a big believer in everything in moderation, and that holds true for both coffee and booze. The benefits of caffeine are widely known, as it can reduce fatigue and drowsiness, but, more importantly, it has been shown to improve endurance and increase muscular strength. While I love my morning cup of joe, I don't want to become dependent on caffeine, so I limit it to one to two cups a day, max. As for alcohol, it doesn't align with my why and it can take away from what I'm trying to achieve, so, for the most part, I don't drink regularly. Don't get me wrong—I love a good glass of wine every now and again. So here is my rule of thumb:

If I'm training and it's a month out from a major competition, I don't touch alcohol; if it is more than two months out from competition, I will let myself enjoy a glass of wine or a Bundy (short for Bundaberg, a local Queensland dark rum) with coke. I also allow myself to enjoy a cocktail or two on special occasions. It is all about coming back to that balance in life.

Sleep

Like food and water, sleep is a crucial component to success. It doesn't matter what you do or who you are, if you are not getting good-quality sleep, you will not be able to give an optimal performance, and that goes not just for the gym or competition but for the classroom or boardroom as well. It is also vital for recovery. Sleep is the time your body dedicates to regenerate tissue, restore hormonal balance, and recuperate mentally.

When I'm in peak training, I try to have a minimum of 10 hours' sleep a night; otherwise, I really feel the stiffness and soreness. And when it's off-season, I get 7 to 8 hours of sleep. When I'm competing, I'll try to get the 10 hours and take naps in between events; however, this really depends on the schedule of the competition. It is crucial at this time to recharge the battery as much as possible before a competition. There is a cool 1995 study by NASA researchers that shows how shutting your eyes for a short amount of time can optimize performance. The magic number NASA came up with was 26 minutes: Called the "NASA nap," the quick snooze (right before deep rapid eye movement, or REM, kicks in) is super helpful in making you feel refreshed without the grogginess, with a 34 percent increase in better performance and a 54 percent increase in alertness.

Even before this NASA study came out, my dad has been a big believer in taking cat naps, and whenever he is visiting, he always encourages me to sleep for 10 to 20 minutes throughout the day. Sometimes I feel like I need him with me all the time so he can remind me to nap, because I get the best out of myself when I do.

The quality of sleep is just as important—if not more so—than the quantity of sleep. Turn off cell phones—put them in another room if you have to—get your room nice and dark, turn down the temperature for optimal REM sleep. Shane and I black out our room so there is zero light that creeps in and it allows for undisturbed sleep—I do the same when I travel and at competitions. Speaking of sleep—I am a big believer in sleeping on big decisions, too. Whether you're a business owner or just someone who has to make a lot of decisions, you'll always have better judgment after a good night's sleep because sleep provides the time needed to remove the emotion, rather than thinking and reacting to the situation right away. I always feel more clearheaded after asleep.

To track my sleep, I wear an Oura Ring, a sleek ring that monitors sleep, activity levels, temperature, and even stress levels. (This is one "biohacking" gadget we use to monitor my body. Shane is really into this stuff, me not so much, but I don't mind being his guinea pig as it all goes back to purposeful training and how we can best optimize our bodies.) I can see all my REM sleep and how often I wake up. If I find something out of the ordinary, I think back on the day and what may have affected my sleep. I also use a heart-rate strap to track my heart rate throughout the day in the aerobic workouts I do. It is easy to get a bit obsessed with the data—I find myself trying to constantly better my results. By prioritizing sleep—the right amount and good-quality sleep—you'll round out the recovery process nicely.

Just as you read about how hard work is necessary to become a champion, recovery, too, is key. No matter where you are in your training, you need to give yourself the necessary time to reboot so that you can get up the next morning and do it all over again. It is an essential part of training—just like your snatches and pull-ups.

Becoming Unstoppable

If you had asked me around 2010 what Shane and I would be doing 10 years from then, I might have answered, "Working in the mines." I still pinch myself every day, making sure the last decade has not been some crazy dream. To see us now and to see where life has taken us, it's phenomenal—but not accidental. The last 10 years played out the way they did because of the daily conscious decisions we made in every aspect of our lives. These decisions were backed up by steady and continuous practice, endless passion, and unwavering commitment to us as a team and our goals.

When I was thinking about how to end this book, I thought about all the times journalists would ask me what kind of mark I thought I had made on CrossFit and the legacy I was leaving behind. But I wonder: How can I possibly know what my legacy is when I am not even done yet? Don't they read about how I am always pushing to the next competition? Don't they see that I am never satisfied? While I am happy with my progress, my potential has certainly yet to be realized.

For the foreseeable future, I will continue to one-up myself and land new PRs every season. No excuses, no complacency. I am often asked, "What was your best year?" My answer always is "My best year is yet to come." And that year may not necessarily mean a year of competition in CrossFit. Maybe my best year will be as a mother. All I know is that I am not done yet.

Instead of asking what I think my legacy is, I'd rather ask myself: What do I think my legacy *will look like*? I know a few things about that: I definitely want it to live on long after I have actively competed in CrossFit, but, more importantly, I want to be remembered as an example of what the body is truly capable of, to be remembered for how hard work, purposeful training, and an unstoppable mindset kept me on top of the podium for so many years. I want to be remembered as a force of nature, of course, but also as someone who embodies true sportsmanship and as a role model for female athletes across all sports. Yes, women can clearly play with the big boys.

So after all this rumination over what my legacy is or will be, I am going to actually leave it up to you: Whatever you take away from me and this book, I hope that it showed someone who loves helping people realize their own full potential.

So, go on, show me how big your heart is.

Are You Doing Enough to Become Unstoppable?

Below are questions I ask myself all the time to make sure I keep on the right track. But at the end of the day, actions speak louder than words, right? So make sure you are always doing the work, and use this exercise as a periodic check-in.

1. What am I struggling with right now? (Identify what is holding you back.)
2. What do I want to achieve?
3. Why do I want this?
4. What do I need to do this morning to set myself up for success today?
5. Have I applied my best self today, yesterday, and throughout the week?
6. What is in my life that is working against me?
7. Is my life balanced right now?
8. Are my habits helping me progress closer to my goal?
9. Am I aligning myself with the right environment to achieve my goal?
10. What's one thing that I can do today that can position me closer to my goal?

SAMPLE TRAINING PROGRAM

If you want to see what works for me in a typical training regimen, check out the following program I use when I'm working toward the Games—it is similar to our PRVN Compete program.

1. WARM-UP, BODY AWARENESS, AND DEVELOPMENT

<u>2 sets each, for quality</u>
60 Single Unders
12/9 Calorie Echo Bike (set at 12 calories for men; 9 for women)
12 Alternating Leg V-Ups
8/8 Single-Leg Box Step-downs
8/8 Single-Arm Dumbbell Sots Presses

<u>Then complete the following, for quality</u>

<u>Parallette Handstand Hold</u>
Accumulate 1:30 or 2:00 minutes

<u>Stationary Handstand Hold</u>
Accumulate 1:30 or 2:00 minutes

<u>L-Sit Hold (Hanging from Rings)</u>
Accumulate 1:30 or 2:00 minutes

Note: Goal is to achieve in minimal sets.

2. CONDITIONING (FITNESS)

<u>2 Rounds, for Time</u>
40 Wallballs (for men 20 pounds for 11-foot target; women 14 pounds for 10-foot target)
40 Toes to Bar
40 Calorie Echo Bike
120 Double Unders

3. WEIGHT LIFTING (TECHNIQUE, SKILL, AND STRENGTH)

<u>Power Cleans from wooden blocks</u>
Every 90 seconds, 4 sets, complete the following:
3 Power Cleans @ 75% of 1 rep max

Then:
Every 90 seconds, 3 sets, complete the following:
2 Power Cleans @ 80% of 1 rep max

Into:
Every 90 seconds, 3 sets, complete the following:
1 Power Cleans @ 85% of 1 rep max

Note: Percentages are based on your 1 rep max clean; this session is not touch and go. Set the blocks to 1-2 inches above the knee.

4. CONDITIONING (FITNESS)

<u>For Time</u>
9 Power Cleans, 215 pounds /150 pounds
9 Front Squats
18 Bar Muscle-Ups
7 Power Cleans
7 Front Squats
14 Bar Muscle-Ups
5 Power Cleans
5 Front Squats
10 Bar Muscle-Ups

Time Cap: 15 minutes

5. BENCH PRESS (STRENGTH)

3 Sets
5-3-1 reps

Set 1:
　5 reps @ 70%; 3 reps @ 75%; 1 rep @ 80%
　(Rest is the time it takes to change the plates.)

Set 2:
　75-80-85%
　(Rest is 2:00 minutes between reps.)

Set 3:
　80-85-90% (Rest is 3:00 minutes between reps.)
　Rest 4:00 minutes between sets.

Note: Percentages are based on your 1 rep max Bench Press.

6. GYMNASTICS (SKILL AND BODY AWARENESS)

Tuck Front Lever Hold
4x 8-12 seconds
Rest: 1:00 minute between sets

Upside-Down Dead Lifts
4x 6-9 reps
Rest: 1:00 minute between sets

L-Sit Pull-Ups
4x max reps, one rep before failure
Goal: +4 / +3 reps

7. ROWING (FITNESS)

4x 500m
Rest 1:00 minute between sets.
Rest 1:00 minute (total: 2:00 minutes).

4x 500m
Rest 1:00 minute between sets.
Rest 2:00 minutes (total 3:00 minutes).

4x 500m
Rest 1:00 minute between sets.

Pace:
1st 4x 500m @ 2k+1 pace or Fast
2nd 4x 500m @ 2k pace or Faster
3rd 4x 500m @ sub 2k pace or Fastest

ACKNOWLEDGMENTS

I would like to thank the team who helped me write this book (Shane, Kathy Huck, and Matthew Benjamin). Their input was incredibly helpful in order for me to share what I have learned to help others on their fitness journeys.

Thank you to everyone who has been a part of my own journey; no matter the impact—small or large—it's because of these experiences that I have been able to learn and grow into the person I am today, and it wouldn't have been possible if it weren't for you.

Thanks so much to my family and friends who have been there from the very beginning, before I even entered the CrossFit world. I am so grateful for the unconditional love and support I have received from you all. You have seen the sweet and the sour moments and were there every time I needed reassurance.

Lastly and most importantly, I want to thank Shane again—my best friend, my coach, my husband, and the father of our daughter, Willow. We have been childhood sweethearts since the day we met and you have been the person who has not only shown me how to think outside the box, but you have supported me, loved me, and guided me in whatever aspiration I have entertained. None of this would have happened or would even have been possible without you paving the way, and it really is true when people say: I am so lucky to have found a soulmate like you. You are truly one of a kind. THANK YOU!

I love you! XO

ATHLETIC TIMELINE

2013
I first competed in the CrossFit Open, less than a month after learning CrossFit.
Ranking Worldwide: 5,954th

2014
I competed in CrossFit Regionals, ranking 18th.
Ranking Worldwide: 241st

2015
I rose through the ranks and lost by 40 points to come in 2nd behind Katrin Davíðsdóttir.
CrossFit Games: 2nd Worldwide

2016
I finished 2nd in the CrossFit games again (lost by 11 points to Katrin Davíðsdóttir). I also finished 14th in the weight-lifting competition (128-pound division) at the 2016 Summer Olympics in Rio de Janeiro, Brazil.
CrossFit Games: 2nd Worldwide

2017
I win my first CrossFit Games with a 2-point lead over Kara Webb.
CrossFit Games: 1st Worldwide

2018

I win the CrossFit Games for second year, with a 64-point lead over second-place Laura Horvath. Also competed in weight lifting at the 2018 Commonwealth Games, winning gold in the 128-pound division.

CrossFit Games: 1st Worldwide

2019

I win CrossFit Games for the third year in a row, becoming the first woman to do so, beating Kristin Holte by 95 points.

CrossFit Games: 1st Worldwide

2020

I win my fourth CrossFit Games, beating Katrin Davíðsdóttir by 360 points. I also started training with Australian bobsled team.

CrossFit Games: 1st Worldwide

2021

I take my fifth consecutive win, being named the Greatest CrossFit Athlete of All Time beating Laura Horvath by 256 points.

CrossFit Games: 1st Worldwide

2022

My team qualifies for the Winter Olympics in January 2022 (however, we were not ultimately selected, due to new regulations). I win the CrossFit Games for the sixth time, beating Mallory O'Brien by 113 points and being the first athlete of either gender to do so in Games history.

CrossFit Games: 1st Worldwide

2023

I competed in the Open but took time off to have my baby, Willow, born on May 9, 2023.

NOTES

Chapter 2: Good, Old-Fashioned Hard Yakka: Success Rewards Hard Work and Those Who Dare

38 **Contrary to the popular myth:** Phillippa Lally, Cornelia H. M. van Jaarsveld, Henry W. W. Potts, and Jane Wardle, "How Are Habits Formed: Modelling Habit Formation in the Real World," *European Journal of Social Psychology* 40, no. 6 (July 16, 2009). https://onlinelibrary.wiley.com/doi/abs/10.1002/ejsp.674.

Chapter 3: Feed the Good Wolf: Embrace Failure and Turn Fear into Fuel

54 **Studies have shown that men:** Claire Shipman and Katty Kay, "The Confidence Gap," *The Atlantic*. (April 15, 2014). https://www.theatlantic.com/magazine/archive/2014/05/the-confidence-gap/359815/.

57 **As Mike Tyson once said:** John Branch, et al., "What Scares the World's Most Daring Olympians," *New York Times* (February 1, 2022). https://www.nytimes.com/interactive/2022/sports/olympics/athletes-winter-injuries.html.

60 **Studies have shown that people:** Katharina Star, "How to Overcome Panic-Related Procrastination," Verywell Mind (December 29, 2022). https://www.verywellmind.com/procrastination-and-panic-disorder-2584095#:~:text=

Procrastination%20can%20be%20a%20common,that%20can%20
contribute%20to%20procrastination.

Chapter 6: Perfection Is Unattainable: Stop Comparing Yourself to Others and Embrace Your Differences

118 **Approximately 68 percent of female athletes:** "Body Image Confidential." ESPN. Accessed March 12, 2023. http://www .espn.com/espn/feature/story/_/id/19232937/espnw-body-image -confidential#!survey.

123 **When women get pregnant:** Adrienne LaFrance, "What Happens to a Woman's Brain When She Becomes a Mother," *The Atlantic* (July 16, 2021). https://www.theatlantic.com/health/archive /2015/01/what-happens-to-a-womans-brain-when-she-becomes -a-mother/384179/.

Chapter 9: Sharpen the Sword: No Thinking, Especially No Negative Thinking

179 **According to a 2013 article:** Hyun-Jun Kim, et al., "Effects of Oxygen Concentration and Flow Rate on Cognitive Ability and Physiological Responses in the Elderly," *Neural Regeneration Research*, 8, no. 3 (January 25, 2013): 264–69. https://www.ncbi.nlm .nih.gov/pmc/articles/PMC4107523/#:~:text=Highly%20 concentrated%20oxygen%20was%20found,increases%5B7 %2C11%5D.

Chapter 10: Give It a Rest: Recovery Is Key for the Body and the Mind

202 **We'll focus on what is called:** Bridie Wilkins, "Zone 2 Training Guide: What Is It, Benefits + Examples," *Women's Health* (February 10, 2023). https://www.womenshealthmag.com/uk /fitness/a42824841/zone-2-training/.

206 **It also has been shown:** Zee Krstic, "All the Ways Ice Baths Can Benefit Physical Wellness, According to Orthopedic Experts"

Good Housekeeping (March 31, 2021). https://www.goodhouse keeping.com/health/a35994614/ice-baths-benefits.

Sara Lindberg, "Ice Bath Benefits: Research, Tips, and More," *Healthline* (April 9, 2019). https://www.healthline.com/health /exercise-fitness/ice-bath-benefits.

219 **If you drink more than what your kidneys can handle:** Joseph G. Verbalis, "Advice | Ask a Doctor: What Happens If I Drink Too Much Water?" *Washington Post* (October 24, 2022). https://www .washingtonpost.com/wellness/2022/10/24/drinking-too-much -water-hyponatremia/.

219 **A mild form may cause confusion:** "Water Intoxication: What Happens When You Drink Too Much Water?" *Medical News Today* Accessed March 12, 2023. https://www.medicalnewstoday .com/articles/318619.

220 **The benefits of caffeine are widely known:** James Morehen, "Caffeine and Sports Performance: Pros, Cons and Considerations," *Science for Sport* (May 25, 2022). https://www.scienceforsport.com /caffeine-and-sports-performance-pros-cons-and-considerations/.

221 **It doesn't matter what you do:** Andrew M. Watson, "Sleep and Athletic Performance," *Current Sports Medicine Reports* 16, no. 6 (2017): 413–18. https://doi.org/10.1249/jsr.0000000000000418.

221 **Called the "NASA nap," the quick snooze:** Tom Geoghegan, "Who, What, Why: How Long Is the Ideal Nap?" *BBC News* (April 28, 2011). https://www.bbc.com/news/world-us-canada -13232034.